CLOUDY
BLESSINGS

Yorkshire Publishing
TULSA

ISBN: 978-1-954095-74-8
Cloudy Blessings

Yorkshire Publishing
1425 E 41st Pl
Tulsa, OK 74105
www.YorkshirePublishing.com
918.394.2665

Published in the USA

CLOUDY
BLESSINGS

A year of adventure.
A season of pain.
A lifetime of wisdom.

NATALIE A. TROUT

CONTENTS

DEDICATION

This book is, first and foremost, dedicated to the entire faculty, staff, and students of the international school I worked for in Kampala, Uganda between 2013 and 2014. Thank you for putting up with my insecurities. Thank you for showing me grace. Thank you for the laughs and the tears. Thank you for loving me.

Thanks to Kim for being my rock and very best friend as I moved through the toughest year of my life, thousands of miles away. I'm honestly not sure I would have survived that year without you.

Thanks to my dad for always believing in his little girl, even when, at 32, she decides to move to Africa. Thank you for covering me in prayer before, during, and after my year of struggle in Uganda. Thank you for returning to Uganda with me on a trip that would provide me with so much healing. I love you so much.

And finally, thanks to my mom who went to heaven on February 14, 2021. The biggest heartbreak of my life was losing you. I am able to survive each day without you only because I know you are with Jesus. I wish you were here to see my first published book, but that will have to wait until we are together again. YMM

INTRODUCTION

I began this journey with the belief that my life was about to get really, really good. I had accepted God's call, and I was ready for my life to finally be the incredible adventure I believed it was supposed to be. I was under the impression that when you do what God asks you to do, you can just sit back and collect the incredible blessings. Because I was moving to Uganda to serve God, I believed I was about to be blessed so immensely that I would be overwhelmed with happiness. I believed my life would be a montage of teaching high school English, inspiring students, walking under African palm trees, and accepting the abundant blessings from God that were about to come my way. Life, I was certain, was going to be incredibly amazing because I had accepted God's call.

Spoiler alert: that's not always how it works. That's rarely how it works.

Sometimes, God has something else in mind, even when you follow His call. For me, He lovingly allowed me to be torn to shreds emotionally, physically, and spiritually for the year I was in Uganda. He had to allow me to be broken apart in order to put me back together and made into who He always wanted me to be. In the span of just under a year, I suffered a mystery illness, survived a car accident, was mugged, lived under the highest terrorist threat in Uganda since Idi Amin, and adjusted to life in a foreign country thousands of miles away from friends and family. It was messy and painful. It was also beautiful. While my vision was too cloudy to fully accept God's blessings in the way I imagined I would, I still gained a lot of wisdom from my rocky time in Uganda, and what's a greater blessing than wisdom?

These stories are for anyone who has ever felt inadequate, insecure, or at risk of falling apart. My prayer is that you can learn from my tumultuous year in Uganda, look at your own trials, and see the beautiful blessings that God has for you. **This is not a book about Uganda.** This is not a book about being a missionary. It's a book about blessings we don't always see clearly, especially when we feel like we are completely falling apart.

After each story I'll share a "Cloudy Blessing." Think of these as the wisdom I gained from the experience I am sharing with you, which I hope you can share as well. I learned the hard way that receiving blessings shouldn't be the goal of serving Christ. However, God will bless you with an abundance of wisdom through each and every experience you have, even when your vision is cloudy.

"For it is God who works in you to will and to act in order to fulfill His good purpose." Philippians 2:13

*Some names and places have been changed
to protect the identities and privacy of those mentioned.*

1

A Time to Say Goodbye

I walked through Kim's yard and into her house, tears streaming down my face. As I entered the kitchen, everyone stopped what they were doing and looked at me. I hadn't cried all night at my going away party because we'd been having so much fun. Friends from hours away had come to celebrate me and my upcoming move to Uganda.

"Are you OK?" my friend Elvin asked.

"I just said goodbye to Ray," I said and began to sob.

Everyone ran over to me with sympathetic faces and surrounded me in hugs. Ray was my ex-boyfriend who had become a close friend. Although we had broken up a few years before, lines were often blurred between us, and at the time, I still believed he was my one true love.

It was the first of many outbursts I would experience in my final days in the United States that summer in 2013. The next day, I would say goodbye to most of my family members at a party at my parents' house in Fort Wayne, Indiana. Goodbyes would be said to nieces and nephews, brothers and sisters-in-law, aunts and uncles and cousins, and friends of my parents who had often acted as parental figures in my life. It was July, and I wouldn't see any of them until June 2014.

Why on earth, I wondered, was I willingly leaving the people I loved most? Well... God. And Africa.

I'd always been fascinated with the African continent, its people, and the mystery and beauty that was spread far and wide. My first trip occurred in 2009. I went with Jesus Film Ministries to Niger where we showed a video about Jesus in villages around the Sahara Desert. I returned to Africa in Zambia in 2013 with a friend's church, just a month before I would move there. I had made those plans before I made the plan to move to Uganda. I had never been so excited about where God was sending me and what He was doing with my life. My heart was so excited and overwhelmed with joy that each morning I leaped out of bed and exclaimed, "Good morning, God!"

In the months leading up to my departure, my days had been filled with prayer and praise. I had so much to be thankful for and so much to look forward to. I felt like the luckiest girl in the world. God was calling me to Africa, and I said I would go. I was so sure that life was about to be as good as it had ever been. Clearly, this was why I wasn't yet married, it was because God was sending me to Uganda to serve Him. He was blessing me more than any husband ever could.

"I'm going to miss you guys so much!" I said through tears at the airport as my parents dropped me off. "But this is what God wants me to do."

My parents hugged me for a really long time before they turned and drove away from the airport, and a few hours later when I got on the plane, my emotions went from sad back to excited. *Just me and God now,* I said to myself. I wouldn't have any family or friends by my side. I had to rely on God 100% as I moved myself to the other side of the planet.

Little did I know how difficult this transition would be. My amazing year of living in the center of God's will for my life ended up being filled with a lot of pain and suffering. Had I been more familiar with some examples from the Bible, I would have known that my time in Africa would be likely to be filled with trials and temptations. There would be plenty of blessings, but I was too insecure and paranoid to even see them at the time they happened.

CLOUDY BLESSING: Trust

God didn't promise that following His will would be smooth or painless. I learned the hard way that there would still be pain in the middle of serving God, but that He would help me through it if I would just trust Him.

Paul wrote to the Romans in chapter 7, "Although I want to do good, evil is right there with me. For in my inner being I delight in God's law; but I see another law at work in me, waging war against the law of my mind and making a prisoner of the law of sin at work within me."

I could have written Paul's very words just a few weeks later when I was living in Uganda.

2

A Suitcase of Insecurity

or years and years, and years, insecurity was my thing. It ruled me, controlled me, and made me miserable. It was like a drug I couldn't shake. And then I got help. I got better, and God helped get my confidence level to where it belonged. I was confident in the Lord and comfortable in my own skin. I'd never been better.

I wrote these thoughts in my journal on September 29, 2013 as I sat in my room in my new home in Kampala, Uganda.

Then I moved to Uganda. It's like I forgot to pack my confidence, and instead, I brought an extra suitcase of insecurity. I feel ugly. I am unattractive and boring. No guy will ever be attracted to what I have to offer. I am annoying. My humor isn't funny. It annoys people. I am lifeless and average. Below average.

I am disliked. People only talk to me because they feel sorry for me. In reality, they wonder what's wrong with me because I'm not married. I don't fit in with married women because they don't "get" me. No one does.

No one needs me here. Did God really send me here, or was it my own idea? Since I feel completely worthless here, maybe it wasn't God. Maybe I screwed up, once again, and made yet another stupid life choice.

Things didn't improve after that journal entry. If anything, they got worse, and on October 25, 2013 I wrote a letter directly to God:

Why did you bring me here? Why did you tear me away from the people I love and the people who love me? How on earth is this part of your plan for me? I hate this. I hate everything right now. I hate me right now. I'm tired of life. I don't really see a reason for me to be here or much of anywhere, for that matter. The idea of going "home" is what keeps me going. But seven more months here? I'm not sure I can survive. I've never so seriously considered ending my life like I have here.

Why are you letting me go through this, God? I came here, like you called me to, and this is what I have to go through? I left my friends and family for this?

I don't know what to do. I seriously don't know what to do. Do I isolate myself? Do I fake a smile but continue to be destroyed on the inside? I hate life here. I want to go home. God, you didn't send me here, there's no way. It was a mistake on my part. You wouldn't bring me here to hurt me... would you?

I battled depression in a way I had never experienced before. I doubted everything, especially God sending me to Uganda. I was just sure that I had misread His will, which was absurd given how I ended up in Uganda in the first place.

In October 2012, I had one month left on the lease of my apartment. I wasn't sure I even wanted to stay in Fort Wayne, Indiana, so the thought of signing a year-long lease seemed silly. My mom suggested I move into my parents' house until I figured things out. She and my dad spent their winters in Florida, so I would have the house to myself for at least six months.

Everything fell into place, and as I began to move my furniture into storage, something strange began to stir in my soul.

"There's a reason for this," I told my mom the day my parents left for Florida for the winter. "There's a reason I'm moving into your house and that I won't be tied down to a lease."

"What do you mean?" she asked.

"I don't even know," I said. "I just know that God has something planned. God did this."

It wasn't until five months later that it all made sense.

In the spring of 2013, I grew antsy and knew I needed more from my career. At that time, I worked as a marketing assistant for a wholesale company that made ingredients and tools for the baking industry. It was a fun industry, but I was unfulfilled. I started to think of my love for missions, but was held back by fears of being too old (32 at the time) and being a single female. On top of that, I was paying off student loans and credit card debt. How in the world would I survive financially if I were to quit my job and become a missionary?

As I wrestled with the idea, two different people from my past reached out to me in random fashion. Both said the same basic thing, "God will make a way." They had no idea what I'd been thinking about, and it was a rather surreal moment. I'd never been so sure that God was saying to me, "Go."

But where would I go? I had been to Niger, Africa, on a mission trip in 2009. I had also taken a mission trip to Nicaragua, and I was preparing for a summer mission trip to Zambia. Where did God want me to quite possibly move for the rest of my life?

The next day, one of my mentors told me about a website that might help point me in the right direction. I decided to check it out and visited the website for the World Missions Organization.

"Secondary English Teacher – Uganda."

I read it a second time.

"Secondary English Teacher – Uganda."

I had a Master's degree in Education. I had five and a half years of experience teaching high school English, and my heart was already in Africa. There was no way it would be that easy. Would it? But it was that easy. God made it happen. I had a couple of Skype interviews and waited to hear whether or not they wanted me to teach in Uganda.

One April morning in Indiana, I woke up at 4:30 a.m. with a jolt and saw the flashing purple light on my phone. It could have been SPAM, could have been a new credit card bill arriving in my inbox, but something told me it was something else, something important.

It was an email from the principal at Redemption International Academy in Kampala, Uganda.

"Hello Natalie! We would like to offer you the position of high school English teacher at Redemption. It is a two-year commitment, and you will be able to return to the U.S. in the summer between school years. We look forward to hearing from you and you becoming a part of our Redemption team!"

I was dumbfounded. It had been less than a month since I saw the listing online and applied. All of a sudden, I was offered a job. I got the job. I was moving to Uganda for at least two years, maybe longer.

I couldn't breathe. I began to hyperventilate, and tears streamed down my face. My family. My friends. My precious nieces, who hold the key to my heart. Two Christmases without them. Two birthdays away from home. Two years of life away from the people I love. But also, two years living abroad. Two years of the gorgeous African scenery that stole my heart the first time I saw it in 2009. Two years of serving God. Two years of making a difference. Two years of being exactly where God wanted me to be.

It was a no-brainer. I would go. I would move to Uganda and teach high school English. It would be my "in" to the mission field. After two years teaching, I would probably become a full-time missionary. God was working everything out in ways only He could.

I was happy to serve. I was excited to serve. I thought I knew exactly what God was about to do in my life. I knew I would not be living in a village or serving the poor every day, but I was still sure that God was going to give me the best years of my life in Kampala, the capital of Uganda and home to more than 1.6 million people.

Fast forward to having been in Uganda for a few months, and I was a complete mess. I was anything but happy and joyous, and I was questioning that God had even sent me there in the first place. But as I look back, I am reminded of how God made it all happen. God put the pieces perfectly together for it to happen. For me to doubt His obvious plan for me was ridiculous, but I did. I was in a deep, dark place throughout my time in Uganda. It would take me years to look back and see that moving to Uganda was definitely God's plan for my life, even if my time there looked nothing like I imagined it would.

CLOUDY BLESSING: Strength

We may never understand why God has done something, but we can trust that He will give us the strength to make it through. I didn't realize, at the time, that God was blessing me with an abundance of strength to help me make it through an incredibly scary and painful year. As much as I felt I was falling apart, He was always there giving me the strength to go on. He will do the same for you. It might be the worst time of your entire life, but once you can see clearly, you'll see that He was with you all along, giving you strength.

"Don't you know? Haven't you heard? The Lord is the everlasting God; He created all the world. He never grows tired or weary. No one understands His thoughts. He strengthens those who are weak and tired." Isaiah 40:28-29

I was certainly far from understanding God's thoughts, but even when I felt that I was at the end of my rope, He strengthened me. He is the only way I survived a year in Uganda.

3

Unexpected Temptation

It was my first morning in Uganda. My flight had arrived very late the night before, and I'd slept on my bed without any bedding, using my jacket as a pillow. Apparently, there was a miscommunication between my mission organization and the school when it came to my welcome, so basically there was none.

That morning I met the two young women who would be my roommates for the year ahead. Darla and Amy, both Dutch, were sipping on cups of hot tea, so I figured I should follow suit, even though what I really wanted was a cup of coffee. They showed me around the house and how to prepare the hot tea on the gas stove. Then we all sat down together to chat.

"Do you like to go out?" was one of Darla's first questions.

"Out?" I asked, not sure exactly what she was talking about.

"Yeah, like dancing and things," she said. Amy looked a little worried about what my reaction would be.

I had been warned about this: that there was a party crowd at Redemption among some of the teachers. The last thing I wanted to do was get involved with a party crowd. Not only had I been down that road for most of my adult life, but that's certainly not why God called me to Uganda.

"Um," I hesitated, and instantly remembered a day in English class at Indiana Wesleyan University in 1999.

I was a freshman, contemplating why in the world I decided on a school like Indiana Wesleyan where there was a curfew, no partying, and not even any dancing. I felt like I was missing out on the "real" college experience. As I thought about such things, my English professor droned on about something boring. The cute guy named Seth, who sat in front of me, leaned back and whispered, "What did you do this weekend?"

At first, I was in shock. Seth was one of the most popular guys on campus. As a freshman, I was pretty stoked about him not only talking to me but taking an interest in what I had done over the weekend. I figured Seth was a partier, but there was no way to be sure. At Indiana Wesleyan, partying was something you didn't do, or if you did, you definitely didn't talk about it without fearing the consequences.

"Went to Ball State University to visit some friends," I whispered back. "Gets so boring around here, you know?"

Seth smiled like we had made some sort of special connection. "Yeah, I do know," he beamed. "So, that means you uh..."

He didn't even have to say it.

"Yeah, I party," I said and smiled back at him.

It was the beginning of a toxic friendship that threw me into the party scene like never before. And I wasn't about to do the same with my experience in Uganda. I snapped back to reality and pondered Darla's question about whether or not I like to go out. I didn't want to seem like a weirdo for thinking about it too long.

"Well, kind of," I decided to say. There was great temptation in partying, a temptation that had gotten the best of me many times in my past.

"You aren't, like, against it though, right?" my other roommate questioned. "We like to go out dancing on the weekends sometimes!"

"I love to dance!" I blurted out without a thought. "I think that would be fun."

My roommates were thrilled. And while they presented it as something they did on occasion, it turned out to be something they did almost every weekend at the time. Often, it was something they did multiple times a week. Wanting to fit in and wanting to experience the culture in Kampala, I sometimes tagged along.

Their favorite spot was a place called Iguana. Iguana, which closed down a few years later, was described online as a place for "whites, Rastafarians, Mzungu hunters, and Reggae music lovers." That's pretty spot on. It was unlike any club I'd been to before. It was a bit of a dive, but it was also so dark that you couldn't see much. The men who went there were mainly either young Ugandans with dreadlocks or old white men from the U.S. or Europe. Women ranged from Ugandan, to Asian, to our little group of an American, a Canadian, and two Dutch women. We drank and danced, coming home each time sweating from the Ugandan heat, even in the middle of the night.

I was sucked in. And for about a month, I was taken back to a time when I was a person I didn't want to be anymore. I was struggling because that wasn't why I moved to Uganda. I went to serve God. I went to teach. I went to keep my life on the right track, not go off course again, but there I was, drinking in the crazy clubs of Kampala and arriving home in the wee hours of the morning.

The school instructed us not to even go out after dark, let alone go to the clubs. While I never felt unsafe at any of the clubs and bars we went to, it was certainly risky, especially with the drinking we were doing. Drinking could certainly impair my judgment so much that I wouldn't even realize if I was somewhere dangerous.

With a lot of prayer and some guidance from friends back home, I stopped going to the clubs. This drove a wedge between me and my roommates, but it had to be done.

I was really frustrated. God wanted me to go to Uganda, I was fairly sure of that at the time. I thought that living in God's will would remove temptation from my life. I was so, so wrong. There is temptation everywhere in this world because it is a fallen world. The good news is, God equips us with what we need to face that temptation.

CLOUDY BLESSING: A fresh start

"When one is tempted, no one should say, 'God is tempting me,' for God cannot be tempted by evil, nor does He tempt anyone; but each person is tempted when they are dragged away by their own evil desire and enticed." James 1:13-14

Enticed. I was so easily enticed.

However, 1 Corinthians 10:13 reminds us that the temptation will never be too much. Not only that, but God will provide a way out, and He did just that for me.

In late October, I was given the opportunity to move out of the beautiful house I was living in and into a small apartment. I would have only one roommate, Amanda, and we would have to share a bathroom, but I knew I had to make the move. God provided me with what I needed to avoid the temptation in front of me, and I gained a lifelong friend in the process.

The thing to remember is that it's harder to see the "outs" if you aren't walking closely with the Lord. He always provides a way out of temptation, but it's difficult to hear Him if we're not near Him in our hearts.

Over and over again in life, God has given me a fresh start, whether I deserved it or not. There will always be temptations to be who we were before Christ, but we don't have to give in. We are a new creation in Him. Don't let temptation cloud your vision of who Christ wants you to be.

4

Invasion of the Nightmare Birds

Birds have always creeped me out. Maybe it's because I was fairly young when my mom showed me Alfred Hitchcock's "The Birds," where flocks of evil crows and seagulls attacked people, poking their eyes out with their beaks. Yeah, it was pretty gross.

I wasn't sure how I would handle living in Uganda where there are tons and tons of birds. I'd never seen or heard so many different types of birds in all my life. Most were small and beautiful and made pretty little songs with their chirps. However, there were also marabou storks.

I had been living in Uganda for only about a week when I saw my first marabou storks. We had just finished lunch in downtown Kampala when I spotted a couple birds walking around some trash, sifting through it as if looking for something to eat.

"What are those?" I asked, as I froze in place, fearful of the giant birds that stood nearly as tall as I did. Not only were these birds tall, but they were ugly. Grotesque. Downright repulsive.

"Marabou storks," I was told. "Dirty, nasty birds as tall as humans. Better get used to them. They are everywhere."

And they were everywhere. You'd see them walking around downtown, flying through the air, sitting in trees and on top of tall buildings. There was no escaping the giant, ugly birds. They were like human-sized vultures. Their faces reminded me of a really old, sunburned man who was losing his hair and covered with age spots and scabs. They can grow to be as tall as five feet, and their beaks are more than a foot long. They are nicknamed "nightmare birds." That's how terrifying they are.

One afternoon I was sitting with some students at a picnic table when we noticed some marabou storks walking around the soccer field next to us. If you can, imagine five-foot tall nightmare birds just walking around a high school soccer field.

"God must have been having a very bad day when He made those," I said. "I know all God's creatures are supposed to be beautiful, but I really think we can leave out the marabou stork."

Marcus, one of my students, laughed, but I could tell he had something on his mind. "Don't you agree?" I followed up.

"Well, they might be ugly to us, but they are still beautiful to God," he said, throwing me for a loop. Marcus was an intelligent teenager, but I didn't expect him to think of something like that. It wasn't the first, or the last, time one of my students would lay some knowledge on me or help me to look at something differently.

I started thinking about how we, on the inside, are like marabou storks. Our hearts are sinful and ugly. When God looks at humans, He should see a bunch of marabou storks, and He should be disgusted, but He isn't. His mercy and grace cover us. He sees beautiful lions, striking birds, and all the other animals we consider to be beautiful, when He looks at us.

"Therefore, there is now no condemnation for those who are in Christ Jesus, because through Christ Jesus the law of the Spirit who gives life has set you free from the law of sin and death." Romans 8:1-2

We deserve to be condemned for our ugly, marabou-stork-like insides, but because of Jesus, we aren't. I even think about some of the major characters of the Bible and how "ugly" their actions were, and yet God forgave them and showed them favor. There was promiscuous Samson, Peter who flat out denied even knowing Jesus THREE times, and don't get me started on David, who repeatedly screwed up and yet was still a man after God's own heart. So much ugliness, just like the nightmare birds.

Sometimes I feel like a marabou stork. I think about how my heart can be ugly, and I'm really not worthy of a second glance from God. I can be just as hideous as a marabou stork in my sinful nature, but what makes God's love so amazing is that even though we can be ugly, He thinks we're beautiful.

CLOUDY BLESSING: Inner beauty

In God's eyes we are forgiven, clean, and beautiful. I'm so grateful that my student removed the clouds from my vision as I looked at the marabou storks and only saw ugliness. There was beauty and humility to be found.

I don't think I've ever felt as "marabou-storky" as I did during my year in Uganda. I felt ugly inside, outside, and all around me. I was in a place filled with such beauty, and yet all I could feel and see was ugliness. I had to fix my heart, but it would take years for that to happen. Uganda was just the beginning of my journey to becoming who God wanted me to be.

5

Rides of a Lifetime

There were a few times in Uganda when I thought I might not make it to see the next day, and usually, that was when I was on a boda boda. Or more simply, a boda.

Forget Uber. Forget Lyft. Forget even calling a taxi cab. The number one, cheapest form of transportation in Uganda is by boda. They are also the most dangerous. Basically, you're putting your life in the hands of a stranger on a motorbike. Bodas are so dangerous that members of the Peace Corp weren't allowed to use them for transportation. Technically, my mission organization frowned upon using bodas as well. Naturally, that didn't stop me.

"I'm so scared," I stuttered before my first boda ride. In college one summer I dated a guy who had a crotch rocket, and sometimes I rode with him, but that was 15 years prior, and with someone I knew cared for me and my life. Now, my life was in the hands of a complete stranger.

"I will take good care of you!" my driver told me. "I will not go fast. You will arrive safely."

"Hold on to the back," a co-worker told me. "You'll be fine! It's not even far!"

It was the second day of orientation, and all of the new teachers were going to ride bodas to where we were having lunch. It was only a few miles away, but I was horrified. I followed the rules and wore my helmet, but I envied some of the others whose hair was blowing in the wind as we zipped down hills and around corners.

We made it to our destination with no problems, whatsoever. It wouldn't take long for me to learn that many boda rides don't end up quite so peacefully. There were many times we'd see lifeless bodies on the side of the road beside a boda. These were either hit by trucks or cars, or the driver lost control. There was even a girl from school who was in a bad boda accident. Not only did she end up in the hospital for a long time, but after the accident, as she lay beside the road bleeding and unable to move, a group of bystanders robbed her, taking everything in her backpack like her phone, laptop, school books, and more. Bodas were dangerous business for so many reasons.

Although my mother had made me promise to always wear my helmet, I never wore it after that first boda ride. The first time I took a boda without a helmet, it was the most horrifying AND freeing moment I remembered experiencing in recent memory. Luckily, most of my boda rides were with drivers recommended by the school. They knew to not go too fast or to put us in danger. They knew we were more concerned with arriving safely than arriving quickly.

One afternoon, however, we decided to take bodas from one area of downtown to another, which meant using boda drivers we didn't know. They were not concerned with our safety but instead wanted to get us to our destination as quickly as possible. I kept my eyes closed through most of the ride as we weaved in and out of traffic, drove on the wrong side of the road, and even ended up on the sidewalk at one point just to maneuver through traffic. Many boda drivers had no concern for safety.

Various sources claim that there are hundreds of thousands of bodas in Kampala alone, and that doesn't surprise me one bit. While drivers are required to have a license and insurance, many don't. Should you end up in a boda accident, which was very common, there was a chance your driver would leave you to bleed, or even die, on the side of the road, rather than face the consequences of not having insurance or a license. According to an Uganda newspaper, more than 2,000 people were killed in Uganda due to boda accidents the year I lived there.

Bodas certainly weren't forbidden by the government or anything, but they also weren't the wisest choice for transportation. While I personally was never injured on a boda, I knew many people who had been, and it was ignorant of me to not wear my helmet.

"The prudent sees danger and hides himself, but the simple go on and suffer for it." Proverbs 22:3

Avoiding death and injury was a plus given all the boda rides I took in Uganda, but there were plenty of other times in my life where I made poor choices that could have ended in disaster. Drinking too much, drinking around the wrong people, drinking and driving, being alone with someone I didn't trust, dating someone I knew had the potential to be abusive. I was anything but prudent for most of my life, and trust me, I suffered for it.

Why do we so often think we are invincible? We think nothing can harm us. While the Lord certainly looks after us and has saved our souls as Christians, He will still allow us to face consequences of poor decisions.

CLOUDY BLESSING: Prudence

The thrill of a boda ride and all of the risks involved was like taking me back to days when I made many, many poor choices and felt I was invincible. I didn't believe anything could harm me. It wasn't worth the risk, but I am grateful that God kept me safe through all my bad decisions and every single boda ride.

Our souls are saved because Jesus died on the cross for our sins, but we are not beyond the earthly consequences of our poor decisions. Prudence, being cautious about our actions, is a blessing that we might not always see as a blessing. God gives us prudence to make wise decisions, and that is a mighty blessing, indeed.

6

You Don't Have to be in Africa

The first time I stepped onto the Redemption International Academy campus, the sight took my breath away. Lush green trees and singing birds surrounded me. Stone walkways and graceful bridges paved my way wherever I walked. And the flowers. There were multitudes of flowers, unlike any I'd ever seen before. The flowers didn't even look real. I remember thinking how the flowers looked like something out of a Dr. Seuss book. On that first day, I stood in awe of vivid colors and exciting sounds. It was gorgeous. I was amazed. I felt so lucky! And then, I felt guilty.

I went to Africa to serve God. But on a beautiful campus, no less one that was protected 24/7 by armed guards? That was not why people went to Africa. It just wasn't right! I felt that God wanted us out in the villages helping the poor. What would people think of me serving God on what was clearly one of the most beautiful campuses I'd ever seen?

"Declare His glory among the nations, His marvelous works among all the peoples!" 1 Chronicles 16:24

While, yes, God does tell us to serve the poor, you'll notice that in most verses about spreading God's love, God wants us to spread His love to everyone- "all the peoples." That included the students at Redemption, even if some of them were affluent.

Redemption had students from nations all over the world: America, Australia, Singapore, South Korea, Congo, Kenya, Eritrea, Columbia, England, Sudan, and more. Some would stay in Uganda after they graduated, but most would go back to their home countries to attend college. We hoped that they would take their experience at our school and use it to impact the world around them for Christ.

"Go therefore and make disciples of all nations, baptizing them in the name of the Father and Son and of the Holy Spirit." Matthew 28:19

Although our campus was a beautiful oasis on the outskirts of Kampala, we were certainly living out Matthew 28:19 in a major way, making disciples of many nations.

Don't get me wrong. I loved helping the poor in Uganda. I loved our trips to the village where we played with the kids and washed feet at the jigger clinic and our Saturday afternoons spent with the babies at the orphanage. But I knew that first and foremost, I was in Uganda for the students at my school, the well-off students with a roof over their heads and plenty of food to eat. They were a part of the group "all peoples" spoken about in 1 Chronicles.

The students at our school were living far from perfect lives. They were, after all, still teenagers, and I learned quickly that despite the differences in race, culture, and backgrounds, teenagers all faced the same sorts of problems. I had students whose parents never came to a sporting event because they were too busy. Some of the female students struggled with eating disorders. Some of the Muslim students questioned their beliefs. Some of the Christian students questioned their beliefs. I had students traumatized by their escape from war-ridden countries to come to Uganda. I had a number of students who lived completely by themselves because their parents were never home; their house help and private drivers were a bigger part of their lives than their actual parents. I had students struggling with depression. I had students dealing with anger issues.

Those kids needed to be loved by their teachers at school. No, they weren't poor, but they needed us. Privileged kids aren't any less in need of the Gospel and good role models than poor kids. Sometimes they're in greater need of it.

As teachers at Redemption, our school was our mountain of influence. It was where we were making disciples. In the same way I didn't feel called to spread the Gospel in villages, others don't feel the need to go to Africa to spread the Gospel. And that's OK! Africa isn't their mountain of influence. So where is it for you? Is it at your job? Your church? Among your friends? You don't have to be in Africa or on the other side of the planet to spread the word of God.

God wants you to serve Him right where you are, and He thinks it's beautiful when you do.

CLOUDY BLESSING: Discipleship

We were created to tell others about Christ, no matter where we are. Don't wait to move to Africa to impact the world for Jesus. Be a witness for Christ exactly where you are right now, showing God's love to everyone you meet. Disciple others into a relationship with Christ. Take the blessings God has given you, and share them with someone else.

7

Speke to Me, God!

Peace could be difficult to find in Kampala. Maybe even impossible. Even our apartment, on the outskirts of town, was a bustling place. The loud music from across the street, trucks driving by, kids playing in the avocado trees or kicking a soccer ball in the neighboring landfill, all made for a noisy, rather unpeaceful vibe.

But we had a place we could go. A place where peace and tranquility were guaranteed: Speke Resort Monyonyo. Missionaries? At a resort? Yes. Missionaries at a resort.

We would either hop in my car or take bodas to Speke, which was about ten minutes away. It cost 10,000 Ugandan shillings to get into the pool, about four U.S. dollars, and it was worth every penny each time we went to our special little oasis just outside the city.

The pool at Speke Resort was the most beautiful I had ever seen. Olympic-sized and crystal blue, surrounded by lounge chairs, the pool was a welcome change from our apartment and all that surrounded it. We would get there early, usually some of the first people to arrive. We'd be very selective with our seating, taking into consideration where we would get the best sun.

Once we selected our seats for the day, it was time to unpack. I pulled out and judiciously situated books, Bible, journal, pen, sunglasses, towel, headphones, and phone. I always paused to glance around and take in my beautiful surroundings. Speke was filled with the tallest palm trees I had ever seen. Sometimes, you could even spot monkeys running around the resort.

"You are welcome!" a woman would greet us once we were settled in. She would hand us menus. I never had to look.

"Good morning, nyabo!" I would say, "African tea with spice, please! Weebale!"

"Nyabo" is Lugandan for "madame." I would have addressed a male as "ssebo" for "sir," and "weebale," is Luganda for "thank you."

Eventually, she would return with a piping hot cup and teapot of African tea with spice, my favorite hot beverage in Uganda. It consisted of black tea, milk, sugar, fresh ginger, and a blend of spices like cinnamon, cardamom, and cloves. On a cool Ugandan morning, it always hit the spot.

Mornings at Speke were pretty quiet. Whether we had headphones on or did our devotions, mornings were a time to relax and unwind as the lounge chairs around the pool slowly filled up, one by one. By noon all of the lounge chairs would have been claimed, and the Ugandan sun, high in the sky, would blaze down on bodies of all shapes, sizes, and colors.

"Think I'll get in to cool off," I said to my roommate.

I walked a few feet to the sparkling pool and dipped my toe in. The temperature was perfect and inviting.

"Just jump in!" my roommate shouted from her seat.

I obliged, jumping into the deep crystal water, surrounding myself with cool refreshment for my skin. I remember one time at Speke some of my friends tried to teach me how to dive. I think we gave many people quite a show as I belly-flopped almost every single time. I never did get it right. My diving days were short-lived.

While the African tea, the pool, and the beautiful palm trees were a delight, the other treat at Speke was lunch.

"Are you ready for lunch?" our pool-side server would come over and ask around noon.

"I'll have the hamburger with fries," I said. "Oops! I mean chips!"

It took a while to adjust to some of the British words and phrases used in Uganda. What we call fries in America, they call chips, and what we call chips, they call crisps. You can imagine how this would get confusing.

I would also order a Stoney, my favorite African soda, to accompany my burger and chips.

We devoured our delicious meal while the sun beat down on our white skin, which would slowly turn red. We would allow another few hours to pass as we relaxed in the pool, and then we would enjoy one more snack before heading home – another Stoney and some garlic naan. I had never even heard of naan before I moved to Uganda. It's an Indian oven-baked flatbread, kind of like pita bread but lighter, and the garlic made it heavenly.

When a day at Speke was over, the day was over for good. Our skin would be fried to a crisp, and we were ready to go home and shower and spend the evening watching a movie on one of our laptops while nursing sunburns with aloe vera.

CLOUDY BLESSING: Quiet Time

Our days at Speke were filled with fun and food, but they were also often filled with the act of debriefing about the week at school and having devotions with the Lord. On those quiet mornings it was the perfect time to read my Bible and pray. Those were some of the times I heard God the clearest, when I could just be still and wait to hear what He had to tell me. Maybe it came through a Bible verse, maybe a devotional book, or sometimes even from another person, but it seemed He always spoke to me at Speke.

"My sheep hear my voice, and I know them, and they follow me." John 10:27

Some days I would give anything to return to Speke to spend a morning there just listening to what God has to say. The good news is, I don't have to be at a Ugandan resort. I can have my quiet time anywhere, and so can you. Take the time to hear God. Know His voice, and follow His lead. What a glorious blessing that God speaks to us in the quiet.

8

The First Day of School

In December of 2011, I packed up my belongings at North Side High School and left the teaching profession for what I thought would be "forever." I gave away nearly all of my teaching materials. After all, I was never going to teach again. Why hold on to all those things?

It was a bittersweet day. I was both thrilled and devastated to leave teaching. For five and a half years, I had taught high school English. I taught for two years in Georgia and three and a half in Indiana. Things had gotten so bad in my particular school system that I was leaving mid-year.

I didn't major in education as an undergrad. I went to college to be a journalist. I received my bachelor's degree in Journalism from one of the best journalism schools in the country, Indiana University. I was one of the lead reporters for the award-winning student newspaper, the Indiana Daily Student. My biggest beat was my senior year when I covered the Indiana University men's basketball team. Any sports fan will know what a big deal that is, and while I had high hopes of someday covering college or professional sports for ESPN, few students graduate and immediately get a job like that. I started working at a newspaper in a small town called LaGrange, Georgia. I covered high school sports for the three local high schools and the local college, LaGrange College. I didn't expect to love it, but I did, especially high school football.

In October 2005, my heart was shattered when a local quarterback was shot and killed. Sure, I wrote some award-winning articles about it for the newspaper, but my heart was so wounded that all of a sudden, sports felt unimportant. As I grieved right along with the coaches and students at Troup County Comprehensive High School, I realized that I wanted to make a difference, to not just write about what happens in the lives of the students, but to actually be a part of their lives in a more impactful way.

Much like when God got the ball rolling for me to move to Uganda, He got things rolling for me to get my Master's degree in Teaching at LaGrange College. No longer a sports reporter, I was a high school English teacher. At the time it seemed like the best decision I had ever made, and the first two years were tough but incredible. Then I moved back to Indiana where teaching was a nightmare. I worked for a terrible school system that drove me so crazy I had to leave. My last day was in December 2011. And in my mind, I would never teach again.

A year and a half later, I was not only a teacher again, but I was a teacher at an international school in Uganda. I'd had a year and a half of teenage-free life. It was great, and it was also sad. I missed "my kids," as I so often call them. My favorite part of teaching high school English wasn't classic literature and grammar, it was spending time with teenagers and guiding them through a tough period of life: high school.

Now, it was the first week of August 2013 and the first day of school at Redemption. I was on the other side of the globe from where I had taught before. All five and a half years I taught in the U.S. I was nervous on the first day of school. But this, for so many reasons, was even more horrifying than any other first day I had ever experienced.

5:00 a.m. I awoke to a mosquito buzzing in my ear. So much for that mosquito net around my bed. I could go back to sleep for another hour or just get up. I tried to go back to sleep, but the mosquito wouldn't leave me alone, and my mind began to race with the typical first-day jitters.

6:30 a.m. I left the house and walked to school alone. The sun was slowly rising, it was cool outside, and I had wonderful prayer time as I made the trek to Redemption. It was so serene as I thanked God for the simple things like the palm trees and sunrise. I walked past large houses surrounded by tall, protective walls, and I also passed teeny tiny, tin houses no larger than the size of my kitchen. I wore a jacket because mornings could be very cool in Kampala before the sun rises. I looked forward to a piping hot cup of coffee in the teacher's lounge before the day started.

7:30 a.m. From the itty-bitty kindergarteners to the towering seniors, Redemption was flooded with students of all sizes, ages, and nationalities. Many of my high school students greeted the teachers they knew. They caught up with each other, asking what each had done on their summer break. It made me think of when I was teaching in Georgia and Indiana, and students would greet me with hugs and high fives. Now, once again, no one knew me. I was just "the new English teacher."

8:30 a.m. The morning assembly was well underway. We sang a few worship songs and prayed. Then the new teachers were introduced. After the primary grades were released, the middle and high schoolers stayed for additional information. My job at the morning assembly was to present Redemption's "Honesty Policy," which was about plagiarism and cheating. This would be the first time I was in front of the entire high school and middle school, so I knew I had to make a splash. I included some funny memes and cartoons about plagiarism and cheating in my presentation, and I was able to keep their attention as we went through the policy. I was told by other teachers that I did the best job anyone had done in years, as I was able to keep the students' attention. Hearing that gave me a little boost of confidence going into the day.

9:45 a.m. The kids already impressed me. The high school was divided into four teams for "team building" out on the basketball courts. They played games against each other as they got to know their new classmates. There were about 60 students in the high school.

10:50 a.m. The cool and dreary day turned into a really wet one. Rain poured from the sky as I prepared my classroom for the 12th graders who would be there in 30 minutes. As if the thunder wasn't distracting enough, the pouring down rain on the tin roof of my classroom made it incredibly loud. Nerves started to come back as I anticipated the seniors walking into my classroom. There were only ten of them, but before they came in, I started to feel like a little kindergartner coming to school for the first time.

11:20 a.m. I didn't have a seating chart, so the seniors naturally chose to sit at the desks in the very back of the classroom. No problem- I just moved closer to them. Their home countries were India, South Korea, England, Eretria, the United States, and Uganda. They certainly made me smile a lot with their questions and comments.

12:45 p.m. Six students. You might think that was a dream come true for a class size, but teaching that small of a class can actually be quite a challenge. The good thing was, the junior class was made up of really great kids who had a great sense of humor. They came from Canada, South Korea, Kenya, Uganda, and the one student from the United States was my principal's son. I could tell right away that not only would this group of six be a fantastic group to teach, but that we would have lots of great discussions and build excellent relationships.

1:40 p.m. I sat at my desk in an empty classroom as a gecko scurried by. My day was done. While I had to stay at school until after 3 p.m., my day of teaching was finished. I flipped through the "Getting to Know You" forms I had the students fill out. The kids were diverse well beyond their home countries. Most were Christian, but some were Hindu, Muslim, and atheist. Even after meeting just two classes, I knew I had an incredible group of students. I was just sure of it: the year was going to be incredible.

4:15 p.m. I was more than satisfied with my first day at Redemption. I had said I'd never teach again, but I was so glad that God's plans for me were different.

CLOUDY BLESSING: A perfect plan

I love the New Living Translation of Proverbs 3:6: "Seek His will in all you do, and He will show you which path to take." God had made the path for me to go to Uganda and to teach again, and the only way I knew that was by seeking His will.

Even when I gave away all of my teaching materials in 2011, God knew I'd teach again. His perfect plan is sometimes cloudy to us, but He sees it clearly. Seek God and His will for your life.

9

Unusual Fears

People were worried about me. I'd decided to sell most of my belongings and move to Africa. There are a lot of people in this world who associate Africa with disease, violence, and intense spiritual warfare, but for me, someone who had already been to Niger and Zambia on short-term mission trips, Africa was a beautiful and often peaceful continent. I wasn't afraid of the things everyone else was afraid of for me.

I was afraid of Christian teenagers.

My students in Georgia and Indiana loved Miss Trout as their English teacher, but not every experience I'd had with teenagers in the past was pleasant. The absolute worst experience I'd had was with a group of teenagers at my church in Georgia.

I was around 26 years old when I thought working with the youth group was a great idea. I was in my first year of teaching, and using both my love for God and my love for teens seemed like the perfect combination. I accepted the challenge of working with a group of sophomore girls. I was ecstatic to be a part of the youth group! I would be a mentor for these young ladies, and I figured it would also help ME stay in line in other areas of my life.

The exact opposite happened. I was open with the girls about my past, like my crazy partying days at Indiana University, and it totally backfired. Their allegiance was to their previous small group leader, a young, pretty, married woman they had known their entire lives who was now leading a different grade of girls. Most of the girls in the youth group refused to accept me. My heart was open to them, and they completely shut me out.

It was bad. It was hurtful. My experience was so negative that I ended up quitting youth group and leaving the church in the middle of the year. I felt that there was no reason for me to stay when they refused to let me into their lives and their hearts. I was shattered. I told myself that Christian teens would never relate to me or accept me.

These feelings all came back after I agreed to teach in Uganda at Redemption. Satan tried to attack me by screaming in my ear, "Natalie don't you remember what happened in Georgia? You can't teach Christian teenagers. Christian teenagers hate you! Remember?" Satan is so good at reminding us of our insecurities, even ones that remained buried for years.

A few days before school started, and my nerves were already out of control about the whole "teaching Christian kids" thing, the school told us that we had to sign up for a committee. Our options were: special events, performing arts, enrichment, and spiritual life. I didn't even think twice about it when I heard "spiritual life." I signed up immediately.

And then, Satan attacked me again. "What are you doing? You can't talk to these kids about God! Look at the mistakes you made in life! If they find out, they'll turn on you just like the kids at church in Georgia!"

Satan is such a dirty liar.

Can I tell you that many of those kids at Redemption loved and trusted me? Not only did I make them write essays and read books for English class, but I also told them about everything God had done in my life and what He can do for them... and they respected and loved me for it.

One afternoon with my 12th grade class, we got into a deep discussion, and the opportunity to share my testimony came up. As I was telling it, I began to have those awful feelings and wonder if I would forever lose them if they knew where I once was in life.

But I kept talking anyway. And when I concluded, one of my students said in his beautiful Kenyan accent, "Awesome, Miss Trout. Thanks for being honest. So many Christians lie about the dark times in their lives, but you aren't afraid."

"Forget the former things; do not dwell on the past." Isaiah 43:18

While I thought the students would judge me for my past, or use it against me, they actually loved me for it. They respected me for it. They didn't respect what I had done in my past, but they respected that I had moved past it and had the courage to share my journey.

CLOUDY BLESSING: Victory

What's hiding in your past? Can you use it to help others? It's such a scary thing, sometimes, to open up and be vulnerable. Look at what happened to me in Georgia, after all. That night in Uganda, after sharing my heart with my seniors and seeing their grace-filled reactions, I wondered why God didn't let the same thing happen when I shared in Georgia. The Holy Spirit wasted no time in saying, "Because then, your poor choices weren't in your past. They were still your present."

Ugh. The Holy Spirit just never holds back when it comes to dropping a truth bomb. The Holy Spirit was right. As I talked about my "past" of drinking and partying in Georgia, I was actively doing it. As I talked about how God had changed my life, in reality, I hadn't let Him do that yet. I was a fake and a phony. And guess what? If anyone can pick up on that, it's teenagers. So, the difference between Georgia and Uganda was the fact that I was genuine. I was willing to admit a wild past, admit that I still made mistakes, and that God was working on me every single day.

It is easy to feel defeated with Satan reminding us of our bad life choices. Satan has consistently reminded me of what happened in Georgia so many years ago, how I was rejected, and how I was a phony. But God is always the victor. There is no past so ugly and dirty that He can't erase it and leave you feeling victorious.

10

Tanning on the Equator

"D on't forget sunscreen!" my roommate Darla said before we left the house for a day at the Speke pool.

"Girl, I am going to get a tan!" I said, "I'll be fine with SPF 15. I can't wait to soak up the sun!"

"SPF 15? You need at least SPF 30," she said. "You'll still get sun. I promise. You live on the equator now, and the sun is brutal. It's unlike anything you've ever experienced."

"Yeah, I burn all the time when I go to Florida," I said, putting on my sunglasses and heading out the door. "But then I tan. I have to burn first if I'm going to tan."

Darla shrugged her shoulders, and we headed to the pool.

Being tan didn't truly become important to me until I was in college. In high school, I went to the tanning bed a few times before prom, but that was it. In college, some of my roommates and I tanned excessively pretty much year-round. I worked a summer job at Dairy Queen in Bloomington, Indiana, while I was a student at Indiana University. I had no time to lay in the sun and get a bronzed glow, that would have to come from the tanning bed. In the winter, the tanning salons were packed, especially in the weeks leading up to spring break. I remember standing in line for over an hour just to tan. The line flowed out the door and into the parking lot. One time, the line of students waited in the snow, but that was the price we were willing to pay to be tan. Now, I was living on the equator and prepared to have the tan of a lifetime, and it would be natural, not from bulbs.

It was a gorgeous, hot day, as it often is in Kampala. We started the day off with some coffee and reading before we actually got in the pool.

"You're looking a little pink," Darla told me as the day progressed.

"Yes! That's the plan!" I said with enthusiasm as I admired my pink skin.

"Seriously, you need to be careful, you can really damage your skin," she said, looking concerned.

Once again, I ignored her warnings. I'd spent many vacations in Florida. I had been to Mexico and Nicaragua. I knew the sun was stronger in Kampala, but my skin could take it. And even better, I'd have an awesome tan in a few days.

The day went on, and Darla continued to apply sunscreen while I figured my first application from the morning would suffice.

We got in the car to leave, and I looked in the mirror.

"Whoa!" I said, noticing my red skin. "I really did burn! This is going to look fantastic tomorrow!"

Little did I know that my skin would continue to cook for another few hours, getting redder as the evening went on. By bedtime, I wasn't just sunburnt, I was covered in blisters. Tiny blisters, about the size of a pinhead, covered my neck, chest, shoulders, and arms. I'd never seen anything like it in my life. I also felt sick.

My stomach and head hurt, and I felt like I was going to pass out. I cried from the pain. Darla had tried to warn me multiple times, but I felt like I knew better.

How often does the Holy Spirit warn us about a decision, but we seem to think we know better? We think we know better than the One who created us.

"The fear of the Lord is the beginning of knowledge, but fools despise wisdom and instruction." Proverbs 1:7

Darla had warned me. She'd lived there a year already and knew the harsh impact of the Ugandan sun. I thought I knew better, but sure enough, I didn't. I was that fool who despised wisdom and instruction. That was the worst sunburn I'd ever had, but I continued to lay in the sun throughout my time in Uganda, damaging my skin in ways I didn't realize. Even without another blistering sunburn, I continued destroying my skin. The damage I did was so intensive that I would pay a dear price almost four years later.

"I'm worried about this spot on my face," I told the dermatologist in 2017, pointing to a multi-colored, asymmetrical spot on my cheek, about an inch below my right eye. I expected her to say what she always said, "No, that looks fine," or I would have even been OK with, "It's probably fine, but let's take a biopsy just to put your mind at ease."

Instead, she said, "Yes, we need to biopsy that immediately."

My concern grew as she had a nurse come in and take a photograph of it before they did the biopsy. I'd had dozens of moles removed and biopsied before, but they'd never done that. The results came back about a week later: I had melanoma, the deadliest form of skin cancer. Since the spot was on my face, I was referred to a plastic surgeon who skillfully removed the melanoma in August 2017. I met with an oncologist a few weeks later and learned about checking my lymph nodes regularly. I would have to get full-body checks at the dermatologist every six months for the next three years, and then every year for the rest of my life.

I knew the dangers of tanning in college. I knew the dangers of not wearing sunscreen in Uganda, but I did what I wanted to do anyway, thinking everything would be fine. I thought I was invincible. Sometimes I play the same game with God. I think I know better. I think I know what's best for me. It's an unwinnable game, considering God is never wrong. His guidance is perfect.

CLOUDY BLESSING: God's Word

Whenever I don't want to do what God is asking me to do, I think of my terrible, blistering sunburn and my experience with skin cancer, and I remember that His path, His plan, and His Word are perfect.

"Do not merely listen to the word, and so deceive yourselves. Do what it says." James 1:22

God provides us with a book of wisdom in the Bible. It is our job to soak up its wisdom and discern what it means for our lives. Don't get so clouded by what the world says or even what your own desires are telling you. Turn to God and His Word, pray about what that means for your life, and trust that He knows what's best.

11

A Day Out of the City

My "Africa Mix" was the only CD we had with us. My roommate Darla and I were jamming out to Shakira's "Waka Waka (This Time for Africa)" with the windows down when we stopped at a traffic crossing. A young boy selling bananas approached the car.

"No thank you, sebo!" Darla said to the young boy, who then heard our music and began dancing beside the car as we waited for the traffic police to let us through the intersection. It was a great start to the long day ahead of us.

We had the car loaded with toilet paper, rice, tea, sugar, and soap that we had purchased to take to the orphanage and school in Bulamo. Bulamo driving on U.S. freeways and highways would have been about a 30-minute drive from Kampala. However, with Ugandan roads and conditions, it took us almost two hours to get there.

As we drove, I became entranced by the beautiful Ugandan countryside. Sometimes I felt like I was in the middle of a jungle. It was so different from the bustling city of Kampala. Darla explained to me that she loved getting out of the city. It was where you could really experience the beauty of Uganda. There was a pallet of green cast off from the palm trees and rolling hills. It was truly a picturesque drive to Bulamo. From there we had to do some "off-roading" to get to the orphanage, which was down a long lane littered with lots of bumps and holes, chickens and cows, and of course, children, who would smile, wave, and yell, "Mzungu!" as we drove by.

The orphanage was thrilled to receive the supplies we brought them. I walked around the compound with Darla, and she introduced me to all the wonderful staff and children there. This space reminded me a lot of my mission trip to Zambia a few months prior, and I felt an overwhelming sense of love walking around the compound.

We met up with Bruno, Darla's sponsor child. I'm not sure I should call him a "child," considering he was 19 years old, but he still had one more year of school left before he would go to university. Bruno walked around with us for a while, and then we got back in the car and started the journey to Bruno's father's house.

"Bruno's father?" I asked Darla privately before we got in the car. "Why is Bruno here if he has a father?"

"This is the only way he can get an education," she said. "His parents can't properly care for him, so he comes here. That's the situation with a lot of the kids. Here they are fed, kept safe, and can receive an education."

It took us about an hour to travel not much longer than a few miles. Bruno filled us in on how he was doing with his studies and his plans for after graduation. He wanted to study tourism at university, and with that sweet smile of his, I could definitely see him succeeding.

Darla had told me that Richard, Bruno's father, would likely have all their nicest things out for our arrival. Sure enough, as we walked into their small, dimly-lit home, the couches and coffee table were covered in lace doilies. It was such a small room that everyone's knees rested against the coffee table when we sat down.

We received the royal treatment, as Bruno's stepmother served us ice-cold Cokes. Bruno's little brother, Peace, was pretty overwhelmed by two Mzungus in the house, but he offered us a huge smile when Darla handed him the toy car we had gotten for him when we shopped for supplies earlier in the day.

We talked with Richard for a few hours, mainly about his profession. Richard was a butterfly catcher. When he has the money to pay for his license to catch them, Richard spends days at a time traveling across Uganda and catching the most beautiful butterflies I have ever seen.

"Then, I can take the butterflies to universities and research centers where they will pay me for them," he said. "If I can just renew my license, it will be very good for my family. Still, I know that God will provide no matter what."

I don't think I'd ever seen someone so passionate about something like that, but what made Richard even more special was his love for God, which was just as apparent as his love for butterflies.

Darla, who was always willing to help others, wanted to help Richard pay for his license so he could get back to butterfly catching to make money for his family. I was more than happy to offer to split the cost with her, and we gave him the money he needed for the license.

After saying goodbye to Richard, Mary, and Peace, we took Bruno to where he could catch a taxi back to school.

To cap off the day, Darla and I went to Garden City, one of the shopping malls in Kampala, and did some window shopping at a department store called Nakumatt. Then, we went to what would end up being my favorite restaurant in all of Uganda: Cafe Javas.

While the entire day was pretty amazing, one of my favorite moments came after we left Garden City. We were stopped at a traffic light when a young, thin boy approached the car to ask for money or food. It was very common for people to approach your car windows at traffic stops in Kampala. Sometimes they would be selling something like g-nuts or sunglasses, and other times they would ask for money or food. This particular young boy was clearly hungry.

"Do you want to give him your leftovers?" Darla asked me, since she didn't have any.

I was thrilled that she thought of that, and I handed her my box of food. She rolled down her window and handed it to the boy who smiled and said, "Thank you!" We were stopped at the light for a long time, which was totally worth it to see the boy sit down in the median, dig into my leftover club sandwich and fries, and smile the biggest smile I had seen all day.

There weren't a lot of times I was able to travel outside of Kampala, but each time I did, it was a special experience. I was so grateful to experience the work God was doing outside of the city, and it kind of made me wonder if maybe I was better suited to living outside of Kampala in more of a village setting. However, that wasn't the assignment God had given me.

CLOUDY BLESSING: God's assignments

"May the favor of the Lord our God rest on us; establish the work of our hands for us – yes, establish the work of our hands." Psalms 90:17

Living anywhere else in Uganda wasn't the work God had for me. He establishes the work of our hands. He designed each of us with specific tasks in mind. Who was I to question where God had placed me and what He called me to do? I was exactly where He wanted me to be.

It won't always be easy, but if God has established what He wants you to do and where He wants you to do it, there is no greater place to be. His assignments for you are made specifically for you. You were not assigned to do anyone else's tasks, just the ones God has for you. What a blessing that God created us for a purpose. His assignments will not only have an incredible impact on His kingdom, but they leave us feeling peaceful and fulfilled.

12

Surgery

On my second night in Uganda, we gathered with all of the new teachers to hear from someone at school about how everything worked. We learned how to get set up with internet, where to grocery shop, how to call for a boda, and what to do if we became sick?

"If you start to feel sick, have a fever, chills and body aches, let us know," she said. "We'll take you right to surgery."

Those of us without a British background nearly fell off our chairs and our eyes grew wide.

"SURGERY?" the new teachers exclaimed in unison, in total shock at the idea of needing surgery simply because we weren't feeling well.

Everyone else laughed, and they explained to us that "surgery" is a British term for what we could call a doctor's office. WHEW.

Sure enough, with my poor digestive system, I needed to go to the surgery only a few weeks into my stay in Uganda. I wasn't the only one. We ended up needing the school van to fit in all of the sick teachers, most of us new teachers. It was possible that we were just adjusting to the food, but the school wanted to be sure we hadn't contracted any sort of parasite.

The bus ride to surgery was interesting. In morning Kampala traffic, the trip could take anywhere from 30 minutes to over an hour. We were all suffering from stomach issues, and the bumpy, dirt roads didn't help with the extended drive at all.

When we arrived, we unfolded ourselves from the van and went into the waiting room. Since we all had the same symptoms, the receptionist asked if we wanted to go in as pairs. Patient confidentiality is not a concern in Uganda. There's no HIPPA form to sign, and we wanted to get in and out as quickly as possible, so we agreed to see the doctor in pairs.

I was paired with Wendell, my friend's husband. We had known each other for about a week. The doctor jumped right in with questions.

"Tell me about your medical history? When was your last menstrual cycle? Is that normal? How have your bowel movements been? What have your stools looked like?" she began.

My face had to be the color of a bright red tomato at this point, and Wendell just kind of put his face in his hands to block it all out.

After going over my symptoms, I was handed a small Dixie cup for a urine sample, a clear bottle for a stool sample, and a paper for the lab where they would take blood. I was shown to the restroom where I would... you know. So, there I was, walking with my urine-filled Dixie cup and stool sample (in a clear container for everyone to see) to the different places they were to be dropped off.

Then came the really tough part. I hate having my blood taken. My veins never cooperate, and I'm often poked three to four times just to get a small sample of blood. Now, here I was, in Uganda, about to have someone take my blood. I was led to a room where I was told to lie down on a padded, wooden exam table. I looked around and saw a few spider webs in the corners, wide open windows with no screens, and a couple of giant canisters of oxygen. I told myself not to freak out, even though I felt like I was in a closet. An unsanitary closet.

Two Ugandan nurses came in and searched my arms, high and low, for a good vein. Then they found one in the back of my hand. They ended up using a butterfly needle that they typically use for infants, and the pain began. They were young, very kind ladies, but it was frustrating to hear them frantically speaking in Luganda, and I had no earthly idea what they were saying.

It felt like it was taking forever. Naturally, my anxiety kicked in, but then something stopped it. What was there to be afraid of? Of course, God had me safe in His arms. Sure, it hurt as they moved the needle around to get the vein, but I had faith that the pain would be over soon, and it was.

That day was the first of many trips to the surgery. It was the first of many blood draws. They ended up typically taking blood from a vein on the inside of my wrist. You know, where there's a big 'ole bundle of veins and arteries. However, there were never any issues. I only passed out once, when I tried to be a big girl and sit up when they drew my blood. I'll never do that again! I also remember the time they were drawing my blood and two men came and began to patch a hole in the wall beside me. I was living in a totally different world than I was used to.

After my labs that first day at the surgery, I returned to the waiting room to wait for my results. The room had completely filled up in my absence. There were people of all nationalities spread from one side of the room to the other. Once one of my friends came out, we decided to get some fresh air. As we did, we saw our driver talking to a young man with both of his hands completely bandaged up and nasty open wounds on his legs. As we talked, we learned that he had been in a boda accident. He went on to tell us how he was a musician and couldn't work without the use of his hands. I told him that I'd pray for him, and I loved the expression of joy on his face when I said that. I felt like that day God gave me peace in that clinic and also to this young man we met.

Finally, after we had been there for a few hours, I was given my diagnosis: food poisoning, bacterial infection, and a yeast infection in my stomach (which most of us had). The doctor said my digestive system was depressed. Poor thing. It was probably sad that it hadn't had Starbucks in a few weeks.

They gave me a massive bag of antibiotics to take for the next week or so.

My many trips to the surgery after that were for various reasons. There was the mystery of spitting up blood. Multiple sinus infections. And, my favorite, the caterpillar wound. I discovered a painful sore on my upper arm one day that looked like nothing I had ever seen before. It was about the size of a pencil eraser, with what looked like one big blister surrounded by dozens of tiny, filled blisters. The area surrounding the central blister was bright red. It really hurt, and I had no idea what the wound was from. A trip to the surgery revealed that it was likely from a poisonous caterpillar. Some African caterpillars are so poisonous that simply brushing up against one will burn your skin. The doctor and nurses lanced each individual blister, packed the resulting holes in my skin with honey, and covered it all with a bandage. I would have to return a few more times to have the wound cleaned and repacked with honey. Eventually the wound went away.

Things were definitely different in Uganda than they had been back at home in America. It took some adjustment to these differences since I faced a myriad of health issues. I was lucky to have one constant I could always count on: Jesus.

CLOUDY BLESSING: Eternity

Sometimes it was tough to have faith in the nurses and doctors at the surgery. Everything was so different from back home, but that didn't make it wrong. It was just... different.

"Jesus Christ is the same yesterday, and today, and forever." Hebrews 13:8

Everything around me was different, but Jesus was the same as He's always been and always will be. Do you ever feel like He's changed? Like maybe He's not as close to you as He was a few months ago? A few years ago? He hasn't changed. You've changed. All you have to do is go back to Him.

Because God is eternal and never changes, we know there's a future with Him in heaven, and that will never, ever change. I had to face many changes and uncertainties in Uganda, but my fear of having my blood drawn or that the doctors wouldn't know what to do, were a waste of time. God was still the same, and that's all that mattered. As the world around us changes, whether you live in Africa or elsewhere, He will always be the same for eternity, even when you're getting your blood drawn while maintenance guys patch a hole in the wall.

13

No Peace for the Wicked

"That's Arlan back there," Melinda whispered in my ear one morning at a church in the village of Kyampisi.

I turned around and saw a nine-year-old boy talking to our other friend. I immediately noticed the scar that extended from the back of his head and around the side. I began to tear up. That was Arlan, a little boy who had survived child sacrifice.

When I woke up earlier that morning, my heart hurt a little bit. It was the regular season opener for the Indianapolis Colts. Sundays at home in Indiana meant church, lunch, and football all afternoon. For me, in Uganda, that just wasn't possible. Instead, I found myself in Kyampisi with my friend Melinda.

The church wasn't very big. Some were dressed in their Sunday best, while others clearly wore whatever they could find that day. Before we even sat down, a little girl grabbed my hand and walked with me to my seat. I asked her what her name was, but she didn't speak English. That's OK. All she needed to read was the smile on my face, and I hoped that my smile showed her some love.

After church, some of our friends showed us around Kyampi-si. We saw houses they were building for families who have been victims of child sacrifice, and we even got to see a house my friend Melinda helped pay for.

It was strange to be in Kyampisi. I had done my research and watched a few documentaries about child sacrifice in Uganda. Kyampisi was one of the biggest and worst areas for this practice. I'd heard about it and read about it, but now I was finally seeing it. Here I walked the same paths where children had literally been taken and sacrificed. Kyampisi is crawling with witch doctors who are quick to tell people, "Bring me a child sacrifice, and you will have wealth and prosperity." Rumors had it that even government officials had used such tactics to try and win elections. Some people will do anything for wealth, fame, or politics, including allowing a child to be mutilated or murdered.

That's what happened to Arlan. He was playing with a friend one day when he was abducted. They not only castrated him, but they also took a machete to his head and neck. They cut out a part of his skull for the sacrifice. It's a miracle that Arlan survived.

Apparently everyone knows who did this atrocious act to Arlan. But the police released the man from custody due to a lack of evidence. This is common with child sacrifice, and that's why it continues across the country and continent.

I got to spend some time with Arlan. I also got to meet his father. We traveled to their village home and sat in their living room. Arlan received medical treatment in Australia after his horrific ordeal, and he had a photo album filled with pictures from his trip there. Arlan was excited and full of life. The only sign of his tragic experience we could see was the giant scar on his head.

I found it emotional to be in this place. Every time a little hand grabbed mine (there were lots) I shivered as I wondered if this child would be a victim of child sacrifice someday. It broke my heart to know that someone could have so much evil in them that they would kill innocent children. Not just kill them, but mutilate them, decapitate them, and then eat their organs or drink their blood.

To me, humans just aren't capable of that. Only monsters. We live in a world full of monsters, don't we? There are sick and twisted people out there, and sometimes it's difficult to see, or even believe, that there's a loving God watching over the world. Sometimes those monsters who do awful things even appear happier and more successful than the rest of us.

"There is no peace," says the Lord, "for the wicked." Isaiah 48:22

What these evil people lack is peace. As a follower of Christ, I know that even my worst sin has been forgiven, and even amidst the chaos of this world, I have peace in my heart. God offers me, and anyone who wants to accept it, that peace.

CLOUDY BLESSING: Goodness

Paul tells us in Galatians 5:13, "You, my brothers and sisters, were called to be free. But do not use your freedom to indulge the flesh; rather, serve one another humbly in love."

Arlan wasn't attacked because God wasn't watching over him. Arlan was attacked because we live in a fallen world, a world full of people whom God granted free will. Our part is to use the love of God to battle those who choose evil.

A few years after returning to the United States, I took a trip to Thailand with Destiny Rescue, an organization that rescues men, women, and children from sex trafficking. On our last night there, we took a brief walk through the red-light district in Bangkok. The evil we were walking through felt tangible. You could feel the evil swirling around you. It was much the same when I walked through Kyampisi.

Evil is real in this world. There are monsters among us, whether we are in Uganda, or Thailand, or even the United States. Make the choice to "serve one another humbly in love," as Paul instructs us to. This is how we can spread peace in an evil world.

Goodness. Talk about a "cloudy blessing" these days. Isn't goodness so difficult to find sometimes? There are little traces of it in the news and on our Facebook feeds. While evil is prevalent on this earth, if we clear away the clouds, we see that the goodness of God is bigger. We are only able to overcome evil by spreading God's love across the planet. Goodness will prevail.

14

Mosquito in my Net

Peaceful slumber on a cool African night. The dogs and pigs had quieted their conversations, and things were quiet just outside Uganda's capital city of Kampala. I had drifted off into a dreamland where Starbucks was down the street and people drove on the right side of the road. (And by right, I also mean correct.)

Eeeeeeeeeeeeeeeeeeeeeeeeeeeee.

My dreams were interrupted by an all-too familiar sound.

Eeeeeeeeeeeeeeeeeeeeeeeeeeeee.

Not again, I think. *A mosquito in my net.*

Beds all over Africa are surrounded by mosquito nets. These nets keep out the malaria-ridden bugs that suck your blood dry and leave you itching for days. What a great invention! But a mosquito net is an invention that can go horribly wrong when, instead of keeping mosquitos out, it traps one inside.

Eeeeeeeeeeeeeeeeeeeeeeeeeeeee.

She was near my ear, and I heard her getting closer.

Eeeeeeeeeeeeeeeeeeeeeeeeeeeee.

I swatted. It got quiet. I wondered if maybe I'd knocked her unconscious.

I returned to my slumber.

Eeeeeeeeeeeeeeeeeeeeeeeeeeeee.

Ugh! I thought. *Go away! Leave me alone! Just let me sleep! I have to get up in a few hours and go to work!*

I was too tired to fully devise a sensible plan of attack. I thought about getting out of bed, hoping the mosquito would get out as well, but then I would run the risk of actually inviting more mosquitos inside the net.

Eeeeeeeeeeee. She would NOT leave me alone.

Too tired to get up, I grabbed my pillow and covered my head and pulled my bedsheet up as high as it would go.

Silence. I had eluded an attack by covering my entire body so she could not feast on my blood. I felt good about the idea... and I started to fall... fast... asl...

EEEEEEEeeeeeeeee!

She had somehow made her way into a small pocket of air under my pillow and was once again tormenting me. I quickly sat up and violently flailed my pillow around me while still inside my mosquito net. I believed that this action would surely knock her around or at least shut her up.

EEEEEEEEEE!

She had only gotten louder! By the sounds of things, she had to weigh at least a couple of pounds. How could she not? There was no way something so small could be making such a loud and annoying sound!

Frustrated with the mosquito's refusal to leave me alone, I hopped out of bed and lifted up my net, hoping she would come with me so I could then sneak back in.

Quiet.

I wait.

Quiet.

And then I saw her. She was big, she was juicy, and she was quietly resting, hanging upside down on the inside of my net. I devised a plan to close in on the mosquito and squish her between the palms of my hands and the net. My mind reeled as I moved in for the kill.

Girl, you are going down! I'll show you not to mess with this American! She surely had a good life flying around Uganda and tormenting people for a taste of their blood. Man, she's big. Is this even a mosquito or some other flesh-eating African bug? She is massive! Why is she so big? I've never seen such a huge mosquito in all my….

SMASH!

I got her. I opened my hands to a blood bath. A large portion of my white mosquito net now had a bright red stain. This mosquito must have enjoyed the feast of her life before her untimely death. At some point the next day, I would begin to itch somewhere and discover exactly where she had taken her last meal.

Mosquitoes weren't the only pesky insects in Uganda. There were massive flying cockroaches that my roommate and I often chased around our apartment with a can of Doom, Uganda's version of Raid. There were millipedes bigger than my hand. I also dealt with bed bugs at one point, who feasted on my legs overnight and left tiny, itchy bites all over. And we can't forget the poisonous caterpillars. Many of my moments in Uganda with these various and exotic bugs were pretty dramatic.

But so were my moments with other people.

And within myself.

CLOUDY BLESSING: Peace

The pesky feelings of insecurity I battled were just like that mosquito in my net, constantly circling my head, making me feel like it was next to impossible to focus on anything else, let alone relax.

"Peace I leave with you, My peace I give to you; not as the world gives do I give to you. Let not your heart be troubled, neither let it be afraid." John 14:27

I spent much of my time in Uganda feeling restless and on guard for a variety of reasons, but Jesus tells us that He has the peace we need in order to relax. There is no mosquito so annoying that God can't stop, no insecurity or anxiety so deep that He can't heal.

What is the mosquito in your net that you can't stop worrying or thinking about? What's troubling your heart and keeping you from God's peace? Let it go. Open your arms to the greatest peace you could ever experience. Turn it all over to God.

15

Hot-tempered Mess

I wanted to do everything right. I was a missionary in Uganda, called by God, and I wanted so badly to do a good job.

It was the first week of school, and it was lunchtime. There wasn't really a teacher's lounge, so teachers sat in the cafeteria at a couple of tables near the students. There was one couple, Ashley and Edward, who sat with the students. For me, I decided to follow what the other teachers were doing and sit at the teacher tables.

"I noticed that Ashley and Edward sit with the students at lunch," I said to my friend who was in charge of human resources at the school. "Are we supposed to do that? No one else does."

"Actually, they really like it when teachers do that," she said. "It's part of building relationships with the students. Ashley and Edward are really good at that, and if you want to do it, too, you should! It's encouraged!"

The next day I decided to sit with the students. I was kind of fearful that none of them would want Miss Trout to sit at their table, but as I scanned the cafeteria for a place to sit, all of a sudden, I heard a group of boys yelling from the back of the room.

"Miss Trout!" the boys from the junior class yelled. Not only did they yell, but they stood up and held their chairs over their heads until I agreed to go and sit with them. This became an everyday occurrence for the next few weeks. I didn't always sit with them, and they'd make me pay the price by giving me the silent treatment for a while, but I wanted to take turns sitting with the different groups of high school students. I felt honored that so many of them wanted Miss Trout at their lunch table. However, none were bigger Miss Trout fans than my junior boys. I felt like their cool older sister or maybe a fun aunt.

One Monday morning, I saw a few of my junior boys before school started.

"How was your weekend?" I asked them.

"It was OK," one of them said, and then he turned and walked away from me, not even making eye contact. I didn't read too much into it. After all, they were high school boys, so who knew what was irking them that morning. But then class time came, and none of them spoke a word. They didn't participate in class. They wouldn't even speak to me.

Lunch was no different. For the first time in weeks, there was no chanting for Miss Trout. No standing. No chairs above their heads.

"Rich," I inquired when I bumped into one of them after school. "What is going on? Did I do something to upset you guys?"

"No, of course not," he hesitated. He looked frustrated and afraid to talk. "Ugh. It's just. No, everything is fine." And he walked away.

My heart sank. I can live without the attention in the school cafeteria, but what I didn't like was that they had stopped partici-pating in class. Something was up.

I decided to take a different route to find out what was going on, so I asked one of their friends in a different grade. I was right, something had definitely caused them to shut down.

"Another teacher told them they were being inappropriate," their sophomore friend told me. "He told them that they were giving you too much attention, and that some people could take it the wrong way. So now they're afraid to even talk to you. They didn't mean it in an inappropriate way at all."

I was both heartbroken for the boys and furious at the teacher who had that talk with them. The boys were not inappropriate, especially not these specific boys who had hearts of gold and would never cross any sort of line like that. It killed me that they felt like they had done something wrong.

For a few days I kept quiet, but at night in my room I cried and cried, wondering how I would rebuild these relationships with my students, relationships that were destroyed because of a co-worker. Was he just jealous? Did he not like me? Did he somehow think I was the one being inappropriate? My anger grew and grew. I felt like I'd already lost control of things, and I'd only been in Uganda for a few weeks.

"A hot-tempered person stirs up conflict, but the one who is patient calms a quarrel." Proverbs 15:18.

I was beyond hot-tempered, and I was certainly anything but patient. I even deleted the co-worker on Facebook (very mature!). I thought to myself, "This man has ruined my time in Uganda!"

Luckily, I let things settle down before I addressed them. I knew I had to talk to the boys, and I had to talk to the teacher who told them they were being inappropriate. Luckily, both conversations went well. My co-worker admitted he overreacted, and the boys felt better once they heard that I wasn't upset with them and that I didn't think they were inappropriate. The teacher even talked to the boys again and apologized for making them think they had done something wrong.

In the end, everything was fine. I repaired the relationship with my students and with my co-worker. I even added him back on Facebook.

CLOUDY BLESSING: Patience

I learned an important lesson about anger through that experience. That is not to act out of anger when you're upset. If you have to, cry in your bedroom, write in your journal, and, of course, talk to God about it, but don't go deleting people on Facebook in the heat of the moment. Take the time to settle down and come up with a plan. "The one who is patient calms a quarrel." God gives us an incredible blessing with patience. He has patience with us. We should have patience with Him and others.

16

Fredrick

I was attracted to Fredrick the moment I laid eyes on him. He had beautiful dark skin, a nice smile, and big brown eyes. I met him not long after I wrote the following prayer in my journal:

I pray that you keep me focused, Lord. Remind me each day of why I'm here. Show me ways to express your love. I pray, that if it be your will, I find someone to love. But if he would only distract me from my mission, then I don't want that. However, I do feel I can handle both. But only you know.

To say I was excited about a guy potentially asking me out was an understatement. My roommates and the neighbor girls from my first house in Uganda were often juggling guys who had asked them out. They had a plethora of men to choose from, and the girls would tell me stories of others who had met their husbands when they moved to Uganda. So, while my prayer was for God's will, I really wanted it to be that I would meet my future husband.

Dating back in the United States had not been at all successful for me. I'd wanted nothing more than to be a wife, and yet I rarely dated guys who were husband material. I wanted a man who loved the Lord like I did. None of the men I dated did, and yet I held great aspirations of molding them into godly men. However, this experiment seemed to always end up the other way around-they would pull me away from God and His will for my life. I had high hopes that maybe meeting a Ugandan man would be different, that he would be on fire for God, and we would live happily ever after in Africa.

I met Fredrick through a mutual friend who met us out for drinks one night. We hit it off pretty quickly, danced together, and exchanged phone numbers. I was over-the-moon happy. I had finally met a guy. And while I had asked God to not let it distract me from my mission there, it definitely did.

Fredrick and I would go on dates when I should have been grading papers, and we would text when I should have been asleep. We even hung out a few times at the house, alone, which was a huge no-no according to my mission organization (even though we never did anything inappropriate).

"I enjoy spending time with you," Fredrick said one evening over dinner at a bistro not far from my house. "Do you plan on staying in Uganda or moving back to the United States?"

I didn't see that coming. "I guess I haven't decided yet," I said. "Let's not talk about it."

And we didn't. Maybe he knew I would leave. Maybe I knew I would leave. Either way, I just wanted to keep things casual with Fredrick. Perhaps if things did progress and get serious, I would want to stay and start a life with Fredrick. One thing was for sure, I was enjoying his friendship. It was nice to have a friend outside of the "Redemption bubble."

After a couple of months went by, I started to question my relationship with Fredrick. Did I actually like him, or did I just feel pressure to have a boyfriend in Uganda?

"Above all else, guard your heart, for everything you do flows from it." Proverbs 4:23

Was I guarding my heart? In the past I was terrible about guarding my heart. It was more like I put it out there for just any guy to scoop up and smash, and this always left me heartbroken. Since I wasn't guarding my heart, I stayed in relationships for far longer than I should have. My heart hadn't been guarded at all.

When it came to Fredrick, I had to ask myself: did I really believe that he was the man God wanted me to be with, possibly forever? In guarding my heart, I knew that the answer was, "No," especially when it was distracting me from the very reason I moved to Uganda. My purpose was not to find a husband. I stopped talking to Fredrick, and it was like a weight was lifted from my shoulders.

CLOUDY BLESSING: Protection

"Do not conform to the pattern of this world, but be transformed by the renewing of your mind. Then you will be able to test and approve what God's will is – His good, pleasing, and perfect will." Romans 12:2

Although Frederick was a perfectly good guy, God definitely protected my heart. And while I missed the companionship of a dating relationship, God's protection of my heart was so much more important. This also got me back on track with the reasons I traveled to Uganda in the first place. Is there something distracting you from God's vision and will for your life? Get rid of the clouds to see what God wants to do for you. Guard and protect your heart, and make room for what God wants for your life.

17

As Famous as Jesus

One of the first cultural words I learned in Uganda was "Mzungu." The world officially means someone of European descent, but in Uganda, it almost always just means "white person."

People at shops would often greet me, "Hello Mzungu!" Or I'd be sitting on my second-story balcony and some kids would run by and yell, "Mzungu!" waving their hands frantically for my attention. There was even a time at the airport when two adults pointed at me and said, "Mzungu!" Apparently, this was never intended to be a derogatory term, and it certainly never felt like it was. It was just what I was: a Mzungu.

Mzungus were certainly a minority in the bustling city of Kampala. We even played a game called "Mzungu Mine." On the rare occasion that we saw a fellow Mzungu, the first person to say, "Mzungu mine!" would get a point. We never kept track of our points, but it was a running joke throughout our time in Uganda.

Once a month, a group of us from the school would travel to volunteer at a jigger clinic in Nakalanda, an island of sorts in Lake Victoria, Africa's largest lake. It was no easy trip to get there. First, we had to drive to the shore of Lake Victoria in the school bus. Then, we would pile into narrow wooden boats that reminded us of what we imagined Jesus and His disciples would have used. (Thus, our nickname for the boats, "Jesus Boats.") I found Jesus Boats a little scary. As many bodies as possible would pile into each boat, and it seemed like every boat we took sported a leak. We always tried to keep our feet off of the wet bottom of the boat, as we didn't want to touch the water of Lake Victoria. If you came into contact with this water you ran the chance of catching Bilharzia.

I knew about AIDS. I knew about Malaria. I knew about Typhoid and Yellow Fever. But Bilharzia? I'd never heard of it. Once I did, I made sure not to EVER touch the water of Lake Victoria. Bilharzia is also known as "snail fever." Snails living in Lake Victoria carry an infectious, parasitic worm that can penetrate your skin and enter the bloodstream before migrating to your liver, bladder, and other organs. Often, this illness will kill you. We tried not to think about it each time we piled into our Jesus Boats and headed to the island, but it was always looming somewhere in the back of my mind. Don't. Touch. The. Water.

The danger in our multiple-mode transportation to the village didn't end with floating in deadly snail-ridden waters. Once we landed on shore, we'd each hop on a boda, with a complete stranger as our driver, and ride almost 30 minutes over bumpy dirt roads to reach the village. Saying it was "bumpy" doesn't do the "road" justice. The road we took to the village was really just a path beaten into the bright orange Ugandan dirt with holes that seemed to jump out of nowhere.

Still, that 30-minute boda ride was one of my favorite monthly Ugandan rituals. Although scary at times, I found zipping through the wilderness with my life in the hands of a stranger in a foreign land was one of the most beautiful rides I would ever experience. Each time I took that ride with the wind blowing in my hair, I embraced the beauty around me and thought, *I am so blessed. Look at where I am.* I tended to be the most grateful for my life on those scary rides.

Sometimes, there would be almost 20 of us, each on our own boda zooming across the island. Since the rather primitive place doesn't get many Mzungu visitors, we were a very rare parade of Mzungus on bodas. Children would bolt out of the trees to run to the road and yell, "Bye Mzungu! Bye Mzungu!" or simply shout, "MZUNGU! MZUNGU!" and wave their little hands and smile.

We would smile and wave back, and often the kids would run down the road behind us as we disappeared into the dust.

The excitement. The thrill of simply seeing us from afar. It was so huge to them. For a moment, I felt like a celebrity with a bunch of screaming fans who just wanted to be noticed.

And then I thought of Jesus and when He entered Jerusalem on the day we now call Palm Sunday. Mark 11:8-10 says, "Many people spread their cloaks on the road, while others spread branches they had cut in the fields. Those who went ahead and those who followed shouted, "Hosanna! Blessed is He who comes in the name of the Lord! Blessed is the coming kingdom of our father David! Hosanna in the highest Heaven!"

It made me think about how excited the people were to see Jesus, and I felt like I could imagine it as if I was actually there. I imagined it to be much like the little kids running towards the road to see us.

CLOUDY BLESSING: Joy

The excitement the kids had for us. The excitement fans have when they go to a concert. The excitement the people of Jerusalem had when they saw Jesus. What do we have that excitement about? Are we that excited about Jesus? Or have we forgotten what He's done for us and how pumped up we should be? The things we put our enthusiasm in are the things that mean the most to us. Sometimes it's a good idea to reevaluate what really makes us happy and excited. Then we can see where our priorities are.

Those of us who would visit the island weren't anything near all that Jesus represented on Palm Sunday, but I'm hoping that our little "fans" saw more than just a bunch of Mzungus. I hope they saw the love of Jesus on our faces as we whizzed by.

The joy of the Lord is not something to only celebrate at Christmas and Easter. Our lives should daily represent an excitement for our Savior. Sometimes you have to look for the joy, as it can be difficult to find on cloudy days or days we receive bad news. Still, it's there. Let the joy of the Lord always be your strength.

18

Beautiful Feet, Where Will You Go?

My darling feet have been through a lot. Despite my usually polished toenails and pedicured soles, my feet have seen some bad days.

I remember a day at church camp when I was in the fourth grade, and I dropped a can of Faygo Red Pop on my right foot. The edge of the can smashed into my pinky toe and squished it into the cement. It burst a blood vessel and hurt like crazy. Ouch.

I remember having warts removed from my feet multiple times as a child.

Then there was the incident when I hurt my toe getting into a boat. It turned nice shades of blue and purple, and I was in pain for more than six months. A few years later I would break another toe after sitting on the couch wrong. Yes, it's possible.

We put our feet through a lot, but we have no idea what some people go through simply because they don't have shoes. As someone with an embarrassing number of shoes, it's difficult for me to imagine a life without any shoes. It's certainly difficult to imagine how shoes can save lives.

Once a month a group from the school would volunteer at a jigger clinic. Jiggers are parasitic insects that burrow deep into the skin, lay eggs, and cause infections and sometimes death. The people living in the village had no shoes, making it easy for jiggers to burrow into the bottoms of their feet, especially in their dirt-floored homes.

We each had different roles at the jigger clinic. I was at the very first station for someone who came to the jigger clinic. I would sit on the ground with a basin of water and anti-bacterial soap in front of me and hold a washcloth.

"Oli Otya!" That's the Luganda greeting I would say to each person who sat on the bench in front of me and put their feet in the basin. The conversation usually stopped there, as in this particular village, no one really spoke English. I washed the feet of some men and women, but mainly children. My favorite part was when my feet washing would tickle them, and they would laugh uncontrollably. The beautiful thing about laughter is that it's the same in every language- no translation necessary.

I saw all kinds of feet on those days. Some feet were smooth but dirty. I'd wash those feet, dry them, give the person a sticker, and point them in the direction of where to go to get their new pair of shoes. But other feet weren't so fine. Most of the feet I washed were covered in scabs and jiggers. Toes were often unrecognizable due to fungus and dead toenails so black that they would sometimes fall off into my hands. I'll refrain from going into too much detail about what I saw, but feel free to look up "jigger feet" online if you're curious. Don't say I didn't warn you.

As I washed their feet, if they did indeed have jiggers, I would finish washing, dry their feet, and then send them into the clinic for jigger removal, where some of my brave co-workers removed the bugs using safety pins and razor blades. Better them than me, as their jobs involved a lot of blood and other bodily fluids oozing out as they removed the jiggers from deep within the skin.

On one of our visits to the village, I performed the task of holding the children as their jiggers were removed. I specifically remember holding one little girl, probably around six years old. I squeezed her tightly, partially to hold her still while the jiggers were removed, but even more so I held her tight to show her love and comfort. She cried and screamed in agony. I shed a few tears, too. I knew this had to be done for her health, but it was so hard to listen to her screams. I can't imagine what it was like to be her, having a stranger dig into her feet with razor blades.

However, my usual job was washing feet. You might assume that washing feet so infested with disease (including HIV and AIDS) and fungus would leave us disgusted and scared, or that the unnatural color of fluids coming out of someone's foot would make us gag, but we weren't disgusted. We weren't even scared. For me, I was heartbroken. So, I prayed. I prayed for the little feet of the toddlers, the teenagers, and the adults whose feet I washed, and I prayed that I wouldn't see them with the same issues when we returned the following month. There was always the chance that they would sell the shoes we gave them. That happened quite a bit.

The Bible talks a lot about our feet and the paths we travel. Whether our feet are perfectly pedicured or filled with jiggers, how our lives end up are all dependent on where we allow our feet to take us.

"My steps have held fast to Your paths. My feet have not slipped." Psalms 17:5

"I have restrained my feet from every evil way, that I may keep Your word." Psalms 119:101

"Watch the path of your feet and all your ways will be established. Do not turn to the right nor to the left; turn your foot from evil." Proverbs 4:26-27

In order for the beautiful African people in the village to stay healthy, they must take proper care of their feet by washing them and wearing shoes. Their feet simply can't be ignored. We need to do the same thing with our lives when it comes to where we allow our feet to take us.

CLOUDY BLESSING: Leadership

Each of us has a choice. We can allow our feet to stay dirty and become infected, or we can take care of our feet and wash them clean. We can allow our feet to lead us to evil, or we can allow our feet to lead us to Christ and place us on the path He has laid out for us.

"Watch the path of your feet and all your ways will be established." Proverbs 4:26

You might not have jiggers or fungus all over your feet. You might even have the most beautiful feet on the planet. But if your feet aren't leading you on a path towards serving Christ, none of that matters. We are blessed with leaders all around us who will help point us in the direction of Christ and where He wants to lead us. Even beyond that, we have God and the Holy Spirit to lead the way.

19

Intimidating Worship

"I will not dance." There was a time in my life when I signed on the dotted line, promising that I would not dance. Dancing was a sin. Those of us who attended Indiana Wesleyan University had to promise to refrain from dancing. No matter what. There was even a joke around campus that we weren't allowed to have premarital sex because it could lead to dancing.

I recall a night when my roommates and I were dancing around our dorm room to Enrique Iglesias' "Bailamos," and our RA came by and made us stop.

For the first time in my life, dancing was wrong.

Dance had been important to me since I was in the first grade. I started taking tap, ballet, and jazz at Christine's School of Dance in St. Marys, Ohio. In the third grade, I was a good enough dancer that my dance teacher invited me to be on the competition dance team. However, this was a huge commitment of time and money, and my parents wouldn't let me compete. Still, I continued to take lessons, and for nine years of my life, I participated in a big spring recital with costumes, makeup, and performances. Then, in high school, I became a cheerleader for a few years. I never imagined there would come a time in my life when I would sign away my freedom to dance. But dancing of any kind was unacceptable in the eyes of Indiana Wesleyan leadership, so dancing was forbidden.

Things were very different in Uganda. Besides singing, dancing was the ultimate form of worship.

I grew up in a traditional church. Hand clapping was pretty charismatic where I come from. I became a little more open in worship when I went to a Baptist church in Georgia. I honestly felt pretty wild just closing my eyes during a song or holding out my hands to the Lord. That was nothing compared to the exuberant, celebratory worship I witnessed in Uganda. Worship in Uganda was the most intense I had ever experienced. And I have to admit, as someone who had attended pretty conservative churches, I found it quite intimidating.

"Come sit with us!" my friend Kristine hollered when I arrived at a worship service hosted by a fellow teacher from school. "There are so many people! How awesome is this?"

"Pretty awesome!" I replied, looking around at the dozens of people piled in the front lawn waiting for worship to start. The crowd seemed to be an even split of Mzungus and Ugandans. It was truly a beautiful sight to see so many people from different countries come together for a Sunday evening worship service. The song lyrics were projected onto a big screen, and a few people played instruments. We sang some songs I knew from America and some Ugandan songs that were in Luganda. We tried to sing along as best we could in this unfamiliar language.

Towards the end of the worship service, things got really charismatic. Some worshipers began dancing and yelling as they praised the Lord. They quite literally looked as if they were on fire for God! And while I was moved by the Holy Spirit during worship that evening, I wasn't feeling a tug to dance or yell. And because of that, I began to feel inadequate. I felt like an outsider. I felt like I didn't belong. I felt like the people around me were so much closer to God than I was. So, I shut down, and didn't get much from the rest of the worship service.

For me, at that time, worship was very personal. The slower songs spoke to me more than the fast songs, but because I wasn't jumping around, I felt like maybe something was wrong with me - like maybe I wasn't as good of a Christian as everyone else. Or maybe, I thought, I didn't love God enough. The people I saw around me worshiped in a fashion so much more celebratory than mine. What was wrong with me that I didn't love God enough to dance before Him like David did in the Bible?

"Behind every trial and temptation is a scheme to get us to doubt God's goodness or our right standing with Him. Who is he that condemns? Not God!"

I found that written in my church notes from a service I attended not long after I arrived in Uganda, and it is so true. The only one who would ever want to make me feel like my form of worship is inadequate is Satan. Not God. God knows my heart, and He knows I don't have to dance or jump to show my love for Him.

CLOUDY BLESSING: Personal worship

Billy Graham once said, "The highest form of worship is the worship of unselfish Christian service." We so often forget that worshiping God doesn't only mean worshiping Him in song or dance. We worship God whenever we do something unselfishly for Him and to help others. Going to the jigger clinic each month was worship. Volunteering at the baby home was worship. There were so many ways I was worshiping God that didn't involve music or dancing at all.

"Draw near to God, and He will draw near to you..." James 4:8

We all do things differently in life, and that includes how we worship. Just because you don't raise your hands or dance during worship doesn't mean you aren't close to God, and it certainly doesn't mean God loves you any less. Worship is between you and God. For you it might be singing worship songs in your car on the way to work, or maybe it's volunteering at the local homeless shelter. Whatever it is, that's between you and God. He knows your heart and loves however you choose to worship him.

20

Spitting Up Blood

I looked down at the sink in horror. There, in the white porcelain sink of my bathroom, I saw a bright red spatter of blood.

It wasn't uncommon for me to wake up in the morning with a nasty collection of phlegm in the back of my throat due to allergies and chronic sinus issues. Even back in America, I would get up, go to the sink, and spit after waking. Never before, however, had it been pure, bright-red blood.

I told myself not to panic and figured maybe my gums were bleeding, or maybe I had some sort of mouth sore. I checked around my mouth and found nothing. I took a swig of water, swished it around my mouth and spit again. Nothing. I went back to my bedroom and turned to the best source for health questions (sarcasm): Google. I was sure there would be an explanation for what I had experienced. All of a sudden, I could taste blood in the back of my throat. I went back to the sink and spit out more bright-red blood. I wasn't coughing. I wasn't vomiting. I was just spitting up blood.

I called my principal so she could arrange for my transportation to the surgery. There were a few other teachers who needed to go that day for other random ailments, which was common, so we climbed into the school van and headed toward the surgery.

The doctor looked around my mouth and down my throat, but didn't see any sores or broken skin. She concluded that maybe I had a cut deeper in my throat, and said, if so, it should heal within a day or two on its own. If I was still spitting up blood in a few days, she wanted me to go to the hospital for a CT scan.

I spit up blood the next two mornings and ended up going for the CT scan, which came back with completely normal results. Then, a few days later, the blood stopped. I prayed that it was over.

It was not.

For the next year and a half, including six months back in the U.S., I periodically spit up blood. For the first few months, it was only when I woke up, maybe four or five days a month. Then, I started spitting up blood in the afternoons and evenings. I never knew when it would happen. I would just be going about my business when I'd taste blood in the back of my throat, and then I would spit up bright red blood. Sometimes, there were even large clots.

I experienced no pain when this happened. I had no light-headedness. Besides my common sinus infections while in Uganda (which didn't always coincide with spitting up blood), I felt fine.

Or did I? I know I experienced a deep depression in Uganda, and I speak of that year like it was the worst year of my life. My mom even asked me if there's something that happened that I didn't tell her about. She just couldn't fathom why the year was so difficult, and why I fell into such a depression.

But I was thousands of miles from home, and I was spitting up blood. I'm a bit of a hypochondriac as it is, always thinking something is wrong with me, and now I was spitting up blood, and no one knew why. No one had heard of such a thing that didn't involve coughing or vomiting. I was suffering from a mystery illness that doctors in Uganda told me to wait until I got back to the U.S. to have checked out. People around me didn't seem to care after a while, and yet every few weeks I went through the trauma of seeing that bright red blood in my sink. No one around me realized how scary and awful it was to face that each morning.

When I got back to the U.S. in June 2014, I was eager to meet with my doctor. I just knew that modern, American medicine would have an explanation for what I was experiencing, but it did not. I saw multiple specialists, had every scope and scan you can imagine, and no one found an answer.

The ENT doctor did a nasal endoscopy. Everything looked normal. Then I went through extensive allergy testing. We discovered I have a slight allergy to dust mites. That wouldn't cause me to spit up blood.

The gastroenterologist did an upper endoscopy. Everything was normal. The pulmonologist did a bronchoscopy. Everything was normal. I gave lots, and lots, and lots of blood. And stool samples. No viruses. No parasites.

The cardiologist had me wear a heart monitor for a month after I ended up spending the night in the hospital due to a severe panic attack. A culmination of all the testing and feeling like a lab rat simply grew to be too much for me. The heart monitor results were fine.

Doctors were mystified. Each doctor who was wide-eyed and excited about figuring out why I was spitting up blood ended up referring me to another doctor, because they just couldn't find what the issue was.

The final specialist I saw referred me to the Cleveland Clinic, but I was tired. I was defeated from being a lab rat for six months, and I decided that I needed a break from everything, even though I was still spitting up blood. About a month later, it stopped.

I never got an answer from any doctor. It's so frustrating to not know why something keeps happening. Even more so, why was God allowing it to happen? And why wasn't He giving me any answers? I had so many people praying for me, but I never found out what caused it, and I probably never will.

Still, I remained faithful. I knew God was with me. He was there for each lab, scope, and scan. He was there with me at each doctor appointment. He was there when the tears streamed down my face as I stared at the blood in the sink, morning after morning.

CLOUDY BLESSING: Faith

Some of my non-Christian friends told me they were amazed at how well I handled my mystery illness, and I was quick to tell them that it was all God. God was giving me the peace I desired.

"People who do not believe are living all around you. Live such good lives that they will see the good things you do and will give glory to God." 1 Peter 2:12

You might not be facing a mystery illness, but you are facing something. How you handle it speaks volumes about your faith and what you believe about God. Are you living as though God's got you, or as though you're spitting up blood with no answer in sight? Always keep the faith, especially when the answers are cloudy.

21

Rain Festival Meltdown

I couldn't find my desk. Amidst the chaotic clutter and madness of Alice's Wonderland that we had recreated in my classroom, I couldn't find my desk. I then realized it was being used as part of the Mad Hatter's tea party.

It was a hot October day, but I couldn't turn my fan on, as it had been turned into a mushroom.

"Our room is lame," one of my freshmen complained as he crumpled up the paper flower he was making and threw it into the trash. "Our book is lame, and our room is lame. Last year was so much better."

For me, that was the last straw. All week I had worked with the 9th and 10th graders to recreate the world of "Alice in Wonderland" for the school's annual Rain Festival. It was a really big deal. Each grade was given a literary theme and then tasked with decorating their classroom in that theme. The night of the festival, children visited each classroom to play games and win candy. Rain Festival. A.K.A. "Christian school Halloween alternative."

I knew all along that it was a big deal, but I never imagined it was as huge and important as it really was to the students and staff. Teachers who had been there before were having massive decorations constructed, and some even hired professionals to cut wood and paint. This was arguably the biggest event of the year, and according to some of my students, our room was "lame." I was a failure at my first Rain Festival.

I thought our room looked amazing. We had the Mad Hatter's tea party, the Queen of Hearts, a Cheshire Cat's glowing eyes and smile projected onto the wall, and even a giant caterpillar made up of two students in sleeping bags. We had truly created one of my favorite literary settings: Wonderland.

Between not being able to find my desk and hearing how lame our room was when we'd worked so hard, I lost it, ran out of the room, and stood behind the giant rock in the courtyard that would hide me and what I was about to do: cry. It was the first time I broke down at school. My kids needed to be doing Language Arts lessons, but instead they were working on Rain Festival decorations, and my room was definitely not up to par with the elaborate decorating the other teachers were doing in their classrooms. I just couldn't handle it anymore.

"What's wrong?" my friend, who was also the school guidance counselor, asked as she walked around the rock and put her arm around me.

"Our room is lame," I said.

"I think it looks great!" Audra said.

I kept crying, partially out of disappointment in myself and partially out of anger for my ungrateful students who were so annoyed with our supposed sub-par decorating job. When arriving in Uganda I was prepared for poverty, prepared for disease, prepared for dangerous situations, but I was not prepared for Rain Festival insecurity.

"The kids think it's lame," I said. "It's not as good as last year's room. I didn't even know we were supposed to go to such great lengths for a festival that lasts two hours. No one told me! I'm just so stressed out, and I want to go home, back to America."

It wouldn't be the last time I was stressed out in Uganda and wanted to go home, but it was the first time I really felt like a complete failure. I was incredibly worried that my room would disappoint my students and my fellow teachers. As a bit of a perfectionist, this destroyed me.

"It's Rain Festival," my friend said. "Who cares?"

She was right. In the grand scheme of things, it didn't matter. Why on earth was I flipping out over such a trivial event? The truth is, God doesn't want us flipping out over anything.

CLOUDY BLESSING: Care

1 Peter 5:7 tells us, "Cast your cares upon Him, because He cares about you."

I'm the queen of freaking out, especially over the small things in life. For some reason, that's just how I operate. But why freak out about things? We can cast every single care and worry on God.

It's easy to feel like no one cares, sometimes. We can feel like we're completely alone with no one to talk to or hear our cries. Our feelings are wrong. The God of this universe has me covered. He has you covered. We really don't have any reason to flip out, especially when our Alice in Wonderland decor isn't up to par.

22

Be Yourself and No One Else

The retreat had been a blast. We loaded all 56 of our high school students into a bus and took them to a retreat center on the outskirts of Entebbe, Uganda. On the shores of Lake Victoria, we fellowshipped, sang praises, and learned more about God and His love for us.

"Miss Trout! Sit with us!" someone would always shout. I felt like I was really "in." The kids were opening up to me, they were trusting me, and they saw me as someone they could look up to. I was thrilled. The retreat was exactly what I needed to feel like I belonged.

It was an incredible few days. From the retreat speaker, to the campfires by the water, to playing hide-and-seek in the dark each night, it was a memorable experience for everyone. I was growing to love my students more and more each day.

Before we left on a Saturday morning to head back to Kampala, we held one last praise and worship session and heard from our retreat speaker one final time. Part of his talk was about lifting each other up. It was about telling people the wonderful things we think about them. He also had us think about what people would say about us after this life is over and we've gone to heaven. Three or four students were selected to stand in front of the room, and their classmates eulogized them.

"She is a really good friend. I can talk to her about anything," one student said about the freshman girl at the front of the room.

"He is a real teammate, and he doesn't hog the ball," another said about his friend.

It was incredibly uplifting to hear the students encourage one another. Then, just as the morning session was about to be over, a senior stood up.

"Excuse me," he said in his British accent. "I was wondering if we could eulogize Coach and Mrs. Rogers."

Ashley and Edward. They were the golden teachers of Redemption. I knew that as long as they were there, we'd all be living in their shadows. I understood, though. They were a fabulous couple with a heart for the Lord and a heart for teens. You couldn't ask for a better duo.

Ashley, Edward, and their toddler, Matthew, went to the front of the room. Students stood, one by one, and expressed their appreciation for the family.

"They are the perfect example of what a couple should be. I want my future marriage to be just like theirs."

"They are so kind. They have us over for dinner, and they just give so much of themselves."

"I can't imagine being here without them!"

It went on and on. Nothing was said that I disagreed with, but something felt like it was stabbing me in the stomach. A nasty mixture of jealousy and inadequacy tore through me.

After that morning session, we were to break off by ourselves and reflect. I wrote the following in my journal:

I need to go home. I am not worthy of being here. God doesn't want me here. This was all a big mistake and a big misunderstanding. If I don't go home soon, I'll just waste more of my life in a place where I'm not needed and not wanted. I thought I had made mistakes before, but coming to Uganda was by far the worst mistake I've ever made.

I was heated. I took the kind things that were said about my own colleagues and friends, and let jealousy destroy the entire retreat for me. I was starting to let it destroy my entire future in Uganda.

"A tranquil heart is life to the body, but jealousy is rottenness to the bones," Proverbs 14:30.

Wow, is that true. No good comes of jealousy. Satan uses jealousy to make us doubt our own worth. A double-shot of, "Wow." And I was boiling over with jealousy as the students praised Ashley and Edward for their kindness.

Why do we so often forget that God made us, and that He made us wonderful in our own way? If we are made by God, there is no reason to be jealous of anyone else. We're not supposed to be anyone other than who God created us to be.

CLOUDY BLESSING: Identity

A few weeks after the retreat, I went to lunch with Ashley. I was honest with her, and I told her how I felt insanely jealous of her and Edward. I told her how it made me feel like I could never be like them. Before I could even finish, she told me about how the first week of school she was scared that all the students would like me more than her. She said they bonded with me so quickly that she was afraid her relationships with them would suffer.

I was shocked. Ashley was worried about me? Ashley was the best! How in the world could she be worried about me? It did absolutely no good for her to be jealous of me. It also did absolutely no good for me to be jealous of her. We are completely different people, and that's how God wants us to be. We were both there to serve the Lord, and God would use us in different ways to do so.

"For we are God's handiwork, created in Christ Jesus to do good works, which God prepared in advance for us to do." Ephesians 2:10

God has gifted each of us with our own special identity. When we compare who we are to others, we can end up traveling down an ugly, cloudy path. Let go of jealousy. Know that God's bright plan for you is the best plan, and it's no better or worse than anyone else's.

23

Not Alone in Brokenness

"It's just been really tough." I couldn't believe the words that were coming out of her mouth. I had convinced myself that she was killing it at life in Uganda.

"I've really been struggling with that," someone else told me the next day.

"I'm not sure I'm doing a good job," somebody said.

I nearly fell out of my seat.

I have this tendency to think that everyone around me has it all together and is perfectly happy. In Uganda, I would see their positive Facebook posts, the smiles on their faces each day at school, and I assumed that they'd adjusted to Africa with ease. I would then tell myself that I was a lesser person because I was not adjusting as well.

There's another lie I often tell myself about other people, especially other Christians: that their lives have been perfect. I believe that they've never made a mistake, that their families have no problems, and that their lives have always been easy.

In high school, there was a girl at a neighboring school who was incredibly beautiful and loved the Lord. Guys loved her, too. Christian guys and non-Christian guys. She was always very kind, but something about her bothered me: she was so perfect. I believed that while I struggled with wanting to be popular and how far I would go to keep my popularity, she was living the perfect, God-centered life. It looked so easy for her. Fast forward to a few years after I lived in Uganda, and she shared a blog post on Facebook that she had written. It was about the physical and sexual abuse she suffered as a child and teenager. I cried my eyes out as I read. I couldn't believe I had convinced myself that her life was so perfect, all the while she was going through the biggest trauma of her life.

I made similar assumptions about the people around me in Uganda. I got to the point where I was so fed up with who I thought were "perfect Christians" around me that I stopped going to our weekly ladies Bible study. A friend of mine knew my struggles, and she told me about something that happened the night before at Bible study.

"Did you know that people think YOU have it all together?" she asked me.

"There is no possible way that's true. People know I'm a mess and falling apart more and more each day I'm here," I said. "It's very clear that I am a mess with no purpose and no idea what I'm doing."

There's a saying that says if someone else talked to you the way you talk to yourself, you'd never stand for it. But I felt like the words coming out of my mouth were true. I was a mess, and everyone around me knew it.

"Not true. Actually, you came up last night. We were talking about our insecurities, and someone said she wished she could write like you. She said she is envious of how good you are with words, and how you just seem to have it all together."

It was difficult to believe, but I knew my friend would never lie to me.

The more I got to know my co-workers and became friends with them, the more I learned that we were all struggling in our own ways. We each had a story to tell. In some way, we were each broken.

There was the girl whose father had died a few years before. There was another girl whose family was battling war in South Sudan. Another had only recently become rehabilitated from drugs and alcohol. And even another who just wasn't feeling the spark in her marriage anymore. Each of us had a story, and each of us felt broken in some way.

CLOUDY BLESSING: Completeness

David, from the Bible, knew what it was like to be broken. He experienced moments of feeling like he was completely abandoned. "I am forgotten as though I were dead; I have become like broken pottery." Psalm 31:12

Everyone on this planet is broken, but only some of us have discovered the glue that keeps us from completely falling apart when things get tough: God's love and grace. I wish that when I was in Uganda I had studied more about David's brokenness and how he overcame it.

Luckily, although David was feeling incredibly broken and lonely, he continued to write about what made things easier: "But I trust in you, Lord; I say, "You are my God." My times are in your hands; deliver me from the hands of my enemies, from those who pursue me. Let your face shine on your servant; save me in your unfailing love." Psalm 31:13-16

It was comforting to know that many of my co-workers who, like me, were living in Africa for the first time, were feeling somewhat "broken." And honestly, it was a beautiful thing. If we didn't feel broken, what need would there be for God and His unfailing love? If we aren't broken, we don't need God to hold us together.

With God we are complete. We are only broken in a sense of this world, and God is the one who holds us together. No matter what the social media updates show, other people are broken as well, and with God leading our lives, we'll get through whatever life throws at us.

24

Birthday Blues

My birthday has always been a big deal to me. I remember having my first big sleepover when I turned 10 years old. My parents let me invite 10 friends over to spend the night. We made homemade pizzas, ate ice cream cake, watched movies, and I got a lot of gifts from my sleepover pals, mainly a bunch of New Kids on the Block stuff. The greatest part of the evening came when my parents surprised me with my very first 10-speed bike. It was white and grey with pink splatters on it, and it had a matching fanny pack on the front.

Birthdays continued to be important to me throughout the years. There was my 16th birthday when my dad took me to a fancy French restaurant for my "first date." On my 21st birthday, my roommates at Indiana University threw me a big surprise party. When I turned 32 so many people showed up for my birthday dinner that we ended up taking up half the restaurant. As a single woman who never experienced a wedding and was never celebrated as a mother on Mother's Day, my birthday was the one day a year I was celebrated, simply for being born.

I was pretty psyched to be spending a birthday in Africa in 2013 as I turned 33. I just knew the day would be unforgettable.

October 22, my birthday, was approaching. My roommate Darla's birthday was on October 25, also just around the corner.

"What should we do for our birthdays?" she asked me. "We should celebrate together!"

"I love that idea! You know all the hotspots better than I do, where should we go?"

Darla knew of a restaurant that had great food and live music. We decided to have our joint birthday dinner there, making it a girl's night and inviting lots of our friends from school.

My birthday fell on a Tuesday, and we did our usual Tuesday evening activity, which was going to a local jazz lounge. The girls gave me birthday cards, my pseudo-boyfriend Fredrick came, and we had a great time as we usually did on our Tuesday night outings. No one paid for my dinner or drinks, and that was OK. It wasn't my official birthday celebration. That would come on Friday.

When Friday arrived, we got dressed up and prepared for our special birthday celebration, three days after my birthday and on Darla's actual birthday.

"Happy Birthday Darla!" people would say as they arrived, giving her hugs. I learned quickly that this wasn't a joint birthday celebration. It was a party for Darla. I had been seriously misled.

At the end of the meal, I could hear our other roommate and our two neighbors discussing, "We're buying Darla's meal, right? It's her birthday dinner, she shouldn't have to pay."

Then, salt in the wound. "Natalie, do you want to chip in?"

I chipped in for Darla's birthday dinner. And paid for my own, for what was presented to me as a joint birthday celebration. There was no celebrating me or my birthday.

I was pretty devastated. I tried not to cry right there at the dinner table, and I held it in until we got home and I was in the comfort of my bedroom. Then, I let the tears flow. For months I had felt my roommates didn't fully accept me and include me, and now this. I had never felt more alone since I arrived in Uganda. It was such a heartbreaking situation that I didn't even feel I could turn to God. I felt 100% alone. I wasn't supposed to experience problems like this in Uganda. Those were the types of things I faced back in the United States – feeling left out.

I recalled feeling left out in elementary school, when all the popular girls made fun of me because of my frizzy hair. I remembered high school, when I was actually IN the popular group, but then they slowly phased me out the summer before 11th grade. I felt like those shouldn't be problems when you're an adult, especially an adult serving God in Uganda.

But the thing is, even though we were all serving God in Uganda, we were still people. Still sinful people. Still sensitive people. People can be hurtful, even when they're Christians. There were also times in Uganda when I inadvertently hurt someone. Whenever there are people involved, things will eventually get messy, to some degree.

CLOUDY BLESSING: Mercy

"Instead, be kind to each other, tenderhearted, forgiving one another, just as God through Christ has forgiven you." Ephesians 4:32.

Be kind. Forgive. It's as simple as that. But let's face it, it's not always easy to be kind. And even when others aren't kind to us, we have to forgive them, because Christ has forgiven us.

I did end up addressing my feelings with the girls the next day. They said they thought my birthday celebration had been on Tuesday. So, I let it go. I was hurt, but I had to let it go.

I had to forgive the girls even if they didn't feel they needed forgiveness. I'm sure there have been plenty of times in my life when people forgave me when I didn't feel I needed it. Forgiveness is difficult, but it is always best for everyone involved. Forgive who you need to forgive, as Christ forgives you. Show mercy, as Christ shows us mercy.

25

Terror Threats

September 21, 2013, was a particularly tough day for Godfrey, one of my seniors from Kenya. Al-Shabaab terrorists had attacked Westgate Mall in Nairobi, and some of his friends were killed. Nairobi was a good 12 hours away from us, but the impact this situation exerted over us was impossible to ignore. Seventy-one people were killed in the ordeal.

Aside from my student losing loved ones, the impact from the attacks made its way to Kampala. The message sent to us from the U.S. Embassy was clear: Al-Shabaab would likely attack next in Kampala. American intelligence believed it was inevitable.

Redemption was the only Christian international school in Kampala, making it a major target for a group like Al-Shabaab. School administrators realized how unprepared we were for an attack like the one in Nairobi, and we quickly began to work with the U.S. Embassy to form a better safety plan. We held lots of meetings and practiced drills in case terrorists were able to break past our armed security at the front of campus. We also prepared for terrorists sneaking in through other parts of campus that weren't so well-protected.

The U.S. Embassy also informed all U.S. citizens living in Kampala that they should lay low until further notice. We were told not to go to the mall or other shopping centers. We were warned away from downtown and instructed to avoid crowds. Don't, they told us, take public transportation. Don't eat at popular restaurants. In other words, stay home. It was too dangerous to risk doing anything else. Uganda's threat level was the highest it had been since Idi Amin, one of the cruelest rulers in world history, responsible for the death of nearly 500,000 Ugandans in the 1970s.

This was serious stuff.

As Americans, there were plans to make. What if there was an attack and things got out of hand? We needed to have a plan. We held a meeting with all the missionaries in Uganda with the World Missions Organization and went over the plan, should we need to make an emergency evacuation. We talked about different meeting places, alternative meeting places, how we would get to the airport, what would happen if the roads were blocked, what we would need to do if one of us became injured in some sort of attack, what would happen if we couldn't get out of the country. The speculation and planning went on, and on, and on. It wasn't fun thinking about or talking about these things. However, it was necessary since the likelihood of an attack was so high.

That first week or so of being in an area of the world facing an inevitable terrorist attack was pretty scary. But then, time passed. Security let up. Fear let up. We began to forget that we were living in an area of the world under threat of a major terrorist attack. And while the threat level only went down slightly, our fear of anything happening had completely gone away.

Trips to the grocery store or the shopping mall returned to normal. Kampala was always vigilant about the potential of bombs or firearms. Even before the terror threats, each time we pulled up to a parking lot, we were greeted by men with large guns. We would roll down the window and chat with one of the guards while the others walked around with mirrors to look under the car. They would also open up the trunk, or the "boot" as they called it, to make sure nothing looked suspicious.

"Do you have any guns or bombs?" they would often ask. "Do you have any bad things?"

"How did you know?" we would sometimes joke.

Then everyone would laugh, and the guard would wave us through. I don't recommend trying anything like that in the United States at, say, an airport, but things were different in Uganda.

When the terror threat level went up again close to Christmas, we were pretty annoyed.

"All I want is a Cafe Javas cheese and tomato sandwich," I told my roommate. "I'm willing to risk my life to go get one. I have to have Cafe Javas!"

She agreed. We got into the car and drove downtown to Cafe Javas. It was so worth it, even though a part of us each felt a little nervous, we weren't going to stop living because of the threats.

Not everyone felt the same way. One teacher's husband was heading to the store for some groceries and wouldn't let her and their son go with him. It was a risk he didn't want to take. As my friend told me, "Since when did a trip to the store require thinking about whether or not you'll come back alive?"

Another friend of mine was debating whether or not they should go to church one Sunday, since they attended the largest church in downtown Kampala. "Then we thought maybe we should all go, and if something happens, we'll die as a family."

Wow. Conversations like that had become a part of my life.

The sad reality is, some people live in countries where that is all they know – a constant fear of terrorist attacks and even attacks from their own military. They live each day wondering whether or not it's safe to go to the store or go to church. We had just a small taste of it.

CLOUDY BLESSING: Courage

"Even though I walk through the darkest valley, I will fear no evil, for you are with me; your rod and your staff, they comfort me." Psalm 23:4

Sometimes, it was pretty hard not to fear evil. I remember a big Christian concert in downtown Kampala that I was so excited about attending. I ended up giving up my ticket because I was too afraid after an email from the American Embassy suggested everyone stay home that weekend. I so desperately needed the Lord to be with me as I felt I was in such a dark valley. Looking back now, it is quite obvious that He was with me the entire time.

I don't know about you, but I don't typically feel brave. I wouldn't use the word "courageous" to describe me, especially when we live in such a scary world. It's human nature to be fearful, especially when terror is knocking at your door, but God offers us the courage we so desperately need. We need only to turn to Him and trust His ways.

26

Mugged

I thought it was going to be an amazing day. A group of teachers had signed up to walk in a 5K to support the Hope Ward at International Hospital Kampala. The Hope Ward was a charity medical and surgical ward for children who needed medical attention. It was a great cause, and we were pumped to participate in the walk. We were also pretty pumped about getting a free t-shirt.

I woke up at 5:30 that morning and rolled out of bed. I pulled on what turned out to be a way-too-small, bright yellow "Fun Run" t-shirt, and I waited for my ride. It was a cool, sunny morning, and it seemed like the perfect day for the event. We would be walking on a route that took us up and down the many hills of Kampala and through a couple of fancy neighborhoods where members of parliament lived. Some people ran, but our group of ladies was just there to walk.

"OK, we must be in the fancy part of Kampala now!" I said as we walked by big, beautiful houses surrounded by tall walls. We even saw a few nice cars drive by, which was a sight we didn't see too often in Kampala.

More than halfway through the route, I was walking and talking with Laura and Kaitlyn, two other teachers from school. My small Ugandan purse was slung tightly across my body- the way we were supposed to carry it. It held my Ugandan cell phone (an old flip phone from the early 2000s), my American cell phone (that I used to take photos), cash, lip gloss, and keys to my apartment and car. I had to have these things with me (ok maybe not the lip gloss), and that tiny purse was all I had.

I knew that being in downtown Kampala with a purse wasn't a good idea, but we were far enough away from downtown that I didn't think anything of it. Downtown, you could have anything from your cell phone to a necklace ripped off your body at any time by someone walking by. However, we weren't in those areas of downtown, so I thought I was safe.

We were in a really nice neighborhood, and there wasn't much traffic. All of a sudden, a boda zipped right by me so closely that I thought I was being hit. It all happened so quickly. As the driver sped by, he grabbed the strap of my purse and yanked it off of me while he drove away.

I didn't even realize what had happened until I saw him disappearing into the distance with my purse in his hand. To this day I can picture him flying out of sight and the horrific things that started going through my mind.

"NATALIE!" my friends beside me and behind me yelled as they ran towards me. "Did he hit you? Are you hurt?" That's how close he got. They were almost certain he had hit me.

"I..." I honestly didn't know. I was in complete shock as I began to take inventory of what, indeed, had just happened to me. "I don't know. No, he didn't hit me, but..."

Then I looked around. Everything, and I mean EVERY-THING, that was inside of my purse was lying on the ground, scattered around the street. Thank goodness for my poorly-crafted Ugandan purse, for it completely busted open when he ripped it off of me.

My American phone now had a shattered screen, but it still worked. My Ugandan phone still worked, and we were able to collect my keys and even my lip gloss.

"I can't believe that just happened," my friend said as I gained my composure and we began to walk again. "He could have seriously injured you if he'd hit you."

"Is that your purse?" someone said further down the street. And it was. The boda driver who attempted to rob me apparently didn't want an empty purse, for there it was on the side of the street, ripped apart from when he tore it off my body as he sped by.

When I really think about what happened that day, it was pretty scary. I was just walking. I was carrying my purse how we were supposed to carry it... and that didn't stop him from trying to mug me.

I'm a big "what if" person, and a lot went through my mind that night as I lay in bed.

What if he had been successful and stolen everything in my purse?

What if he had hit me while trying to steal it?

What if the strap didn't break and he dragged me down the street with him? That's the big one. Being dragged by boda is not something I like to think about, but I couldn't get the thought out of my head.

The "what ifs" could have gone on forever and ever, but what I really needed to do was thank God that the situation wasn't worse.

CLOUDY BLESSING: Soul Safety

"The Lord is my light and my salvation; He protects me from danger – whom shall I fear?" Psalm 27:1

Something worse could always happen in any situation, but thinking about it and dwelling on it won't prevent it. I needed to stop the "what ifs" and be grateful.

The Lord protected me from danger that day. Even if the driver had taken off with all of my things. Even if I had been injured. Even if I had been killed, I would have immediately been in the arms of my Savior. I had nothing to fear.

God is the protector of the number one part of our bodies: our souls. Even in a worst-case scenario, our souls are His. When we face things like cancer, or a car accident, it doesn't mean God wasn't keeping us "safe." All that matters to Him, and should matter to us, is our souls and where we spend eternity. Our souls are always safe with God.

27

Spicy Ginger Goodness

I have always loved pop. For those of you from outside the Midwest, that's soda, Coke, or whatever else it is you call a delicious, sugary, carbonated beverage. Unfortunately, I wasn't allowed to drink a lot of pop growing up, unless it was Diet Rite. My parents loved Diet Rite. The only time I had anything other than Diet Rite was when I visited my Grandma and Grandpa Trout at the lake. Their fridge, full of Faygo Red Pop, was one of my favorite things about visiting.

Once I hit high school and could drive, I could buy all the pop I wanted. I worked at a 50's style restaurant called Arnold's Drive-In, where I discovered flavored pops. I'd sip on a vanilla or cherry Coke throughout my shift as a waitress. In college at Indiana Wesleyan, we would break curfew for pop. Although we had to be in by 10 p.m. during the week, our desire for a fountain vanilla Coke from the Handy Andy gas station across campus was just too insatiable to ignore. We'd literally bust the screen out of our first-floor dorm room, run to my car, and go get our pops at Handy Andy. It was worth the risk of being caught. (For the record, we never were.)

As an adult, I've also gone through many phases of not drinking pop at all. It's bad for me. It's bad for everyone, even diet pop.

But it's so, so good. There is nothing that makes my taste buds happier than a sparkling beverage. Pop has long been an addiction of mine, and it grew worse in Uganda.

My roommates wanted to take me out for pizza my first official evening in Uganda, so we walked to a nearby pizzeria called Café Roma. First, I was blown away that one of my personal pizza options was a tuna and onion pizza. I didn't have to think twice about ordering that. Then, I just assumed I'd order an ice-cold Coke.

"Have you ever had a Stoney?" Darla asked.

"Stoney?" I replied, having never heard of it.

"It's a ginger beer, kind of like ginger ale but really strong," she said. "I love it, but some people hate it."

"Ginger beer? Like, alcohol?" I asked.

"No, it's just called that, like root beer. There's no alcohol in it."

I decided to give it a try, not knowing the sensational power it would hold over my taste buds. I put my straw into the brown glass bottle that read, "Stoney Tangawizi" and slurped up my first taste of Stoney. After I swallowed, I instinctively coughed as a mega-blast of ginger hit my throat.

"WHOA!" I gasped. "That is strong!"

My roommates laughed and shook their heads. That was a typical first-reaction to Stoney. It was a powerful ginger beverage. I took a second sip, and didn't cough this time. Instead, my eyes lit up. I was hooked. Stoney became a serious addiction for me. And like most pop, it tasted best in a glass bottle, although that didn't stop me from buying it in plastic at the grocery store, the only way to buy it outside of a restaurant.

We even had Stoney at the school snack bar after classes. After the final bell each day, one of my students would come to my classroom, "Miss Trout, you want a Stoney?" I'd give him the 2,000 Ugandan shillings it cost for a Stoney, and he would go get me my afternoon refreshment.

One weekend, when I was especially homesick, Darla gave me a gift. It was a bird figurine made out of Stoney bottle caps. She knew my love for Stoney, and the small gesture certainly helped to cheer me up. I still have my Stoney bird. It sits on my desk at work.

I loved Stoney so much that I started taking pictures of every Stoney I drank and shared them on social media. About a week into doing so, I was drinking a Stoney and talking to my mom on Skype.

"Are you sure you should be posting those pictures of Stoney?" she asked me.

I was confused.

"It's just that, well, you're there as a missionary," she went on. "I don't know if you should be flaunting your drinking on social media."

I burst out laughing, nearly blowing Stoney out my nose. "MOM!" I said. "It's not alcohol!"

She was so relieved, and I made sure to let my social media followers know that Stoney wasn't an alcoholic beverage.

Stoney was something that made me feel good. In the midst of one of the toughest years of my life, it offered me an escape. It gave me joy. It fulfilled me.

CLOUDY BLESSING: Satisfaction

When I returned to the United States, Stoney wasn't an option for escape, as Coca-Cola doesn't sell the beverage here. And that's OK. I had learned that the escape and fulfillment of Christ was way more satisfying. Stoney is great. God is greater. Stoney was temporary. God is eternal.

There are many things we can turn to for satisfaction and comfort, but many are harmful, and none is greater than God. I'm grateful that the desire to use men and alcohol as a way to feel fulfilled was in my past. All that the world offers in satisfaction can easily cloud our vision from right and wrong. I encourage you to take inventory of your life to see where your refreshment and satisfaction come from. God should be leading the list, as everything He offers is far greater than anything else. Even Stoney.

28

The Call that Broke Me

"Happy Thanksgiving!" I announced to my roommate, Amanda, as we met in the hallway of our apartment on a November morning.

"Happy Thanksgiving!" she exclaimed back.

Unfortunately, we weren't getting ready for Thanksgiving dinner. We were getting ready to go to work. Since Thanksgiving was an American holiday, we didn't have the day off at school. That evening we would meet up with some other Americans for a modified Thanksgiving meal, but it was nothing like the gluttonous and fun-filled time I usually had with my family.

That night I came home from our Thanksgiving dinner and, naturally, checked Facebook. I was tagged in a bunch of photos with my family, which was odd because clearly, I was thousands of miles away. Sure enough, my family had created a life-sized version of me. They had a big picture of my head that they stuck on top of a stuffed sweater, stuffed jeans, and even a pair of boots. They each took photos with me and even had me sit at the table to play our traditional games of Euchre. It was hysterical, and it also tore at my heartstrings.

As one of my friends in Uganda told me, "Wow, your family must really love and miss you!" And she was right. They did.

On December 13 I knew my family would be getting together for Christmas, so I had a time set up to Skype with them. I went into my bedroom, closed the door, sat down at my computer, and sent the call to my mom who would answer from her cell phone.

"Natalie! Merry Christmas!" she said. I could then hear a bunch of other "Merry Christmas!" greetings from family in the background. "How are you? Did you have a good day?"

"Yeah, it was good," I said. "Who all is there?"

"Grandma Trout, your brothers, the kids," she said. "Pretty much everyone except you! We miss you so much. It's not the same without you here."

"Let me talk to Grandma," I said.

Mom took the phone to Grandma, who was 90 at the time, and tried to explain to Grandma what was going on. She was pretty amazed to see my face on the cell phone and to learn that she could talk to me while I was in Uganda. Grandma then passed the phone on to my dad, and then my brothers, my sister-in-laws, and, of course, my eight nieces and nephews. I was over-the-moon happy to see their smiling faces.

"It's late, and I better get to bed," I said when the phone was passed back to my mom. They were eight hours behind us. I was choking back tears, but didn't want to ruin their fun, so I ended the call. "I miss you guys so much. I love you!"

"We love you, too, Natalie," she said. "Merry Christmas!"

And we disconnected the call.

Talk about heart-wrenching pain. I had been in Uganda for four months before having a complete breakdown over missing my family. And this was a big one. I was a mess. I sat in my bedroom and sobbed at the idea of my family being together without me. They were so, so far away. I also felt sick at the idea that it could be the last Christmas with my grandma. Was I missing the last Christmas with my grandma?

My heart hurt so much. But then I thought of our day guard, a Congolese refugee who had lost a few children to the violence as they escaped the Congo. I thought about the large field of trash across from our compound and the children who played in it. I thought of the guards at school who searched my bags each day with their guns flung over their shoulders, since the terror threat was so high.

Was it OK that I was sad simply because I missed my family? I hadn't escaped a dangerous country or lost children to violence. I wasn't playing in a field of garbage. I hadn't experienced a terrorist attack like the ones our school guards were trying to prevent. Who was I to be so heartbroken simply because I missed my family? Did God think I was completely ridiculous for being so sad on that December night?

"Jesus wept." John 11:35

Jesus experienced sadness. When His friend Lazarus died, He wept even knowing full well that He was about to raise him from the dead. Those two words about Jesus weeping say so much. They show that it's OK to cry, it's OK to mourn and to be brokenhearted. And even more encouraging is the fact that Jesus mourns with us when we are sad.

CLOUDY BLESSING: Empathy

"The Lord is close to the brokenhearted and saves those who are crushed in spirit." Psalm 34:17

Not only is it OK to be sad, it's OK to take it to God. So that night, in bed and under my mosquito net, I cried and cried and begged God for comfort. I eventually fell asleep and woke up the next morning, ready to take on the day. God had delivered.

Jesus can empathize with us because of His time on earth. Even Jesus was sad. He understands when we feel sadness, so it's perfectly fine to cry it out and turn to Him for the peace we desire in those moments. Don't forget His perfect empathy for us and all that we go through.

29

Church and Food

Ifully expected to be a part of a church when I lived in Uganda, but I quickly learned that actually, quite a few people in our school community didn't even go to church. We got plenty of "church" time throughout the week at school, at chapel, and in our Bible studies and small groups.

However, there were many Sundays that I found myself at church. The first church I attended for a few months was across town, where I would go with my Dutch roommates. It was pretty charismatic but always seemed to have a good message. I liked going to that church mainly because it was so close to a shopping center where I could get groceries, and we would always go out to eat at one of our favorite cafes.

Sometimes I would attend the church that gathered on our school campus. That was the most convenient, since I could walk, but it, unfortunately, wasn't near any stores or cafes. When church ended, I'd simply walk home and make something to eat.

My favorite church to attend was Watoto. Watoto Church was a massive church in downtown Kampala. They were known not only for their amazing ministries throughout Uganda, but also for their famous Watoto Children's Choir that traveled the world. Watoto was huge, which meant there had to be extra security. It was almost like being at the airport. They would search our bags before we went in, and we had to walk through metal detectors each time we went.

Besides the incredible music and sermons, Watoto was great because it had a Saturday evening service, which meant we would go to dinner afterward. Sometimes we would go for a sandwich at , but other times, when we really wanted to live it up, we would go to Samari, a Japanese restaurant owned by a family from our school.

My favorite memory from church was the Watoto Church Christmas show, which we attended with almost all of our co-workers on a Saturday evening.

"They're having hot dogs," our friend told us. Her husband worked with the children's choir and knew all about the incredible set up for the Christmas show.

"Hot dogs?" my roommate Amanda said. "I haven't had a hot dog since I got here! That is so exciting!"

We were super pumped about our hot dogs, but then our friend clued us in to another thing to look for.

"Look for the snipers," she said. "You'll be able to see them on the buildings around the church. Watoto would be a huge hit for terrorists, so they're taking every safety measure possible."

Sure enough, as we chowed down on our hotdogs and took selfies in the parking lot before attending the show, we saw the snipers on adjacent buildings. I guess it should have made me feel safer, but instead it gave me a sick feeling in my stomach. We were about to watch a Christmas show in a place that was a prime target for terrorists in the middle of a seriously dangerous time.

The show went off without a hitch, and it was incredible. The music was outstanding, the dancing and costumes were amazing, and they even made it snow at the end of the program. Watoto certainly knew how to put on a show!

Looking back, I'm glad I was able to visit different churches in Kampala. It gave me a taste of the different types of worship and lessons that one could experience, even though I did tend to base my visits over whether or not I could get a good meal afterwards.

CLOUDY BLESSING: Nourishment

Oh, how I love food! While we should certainly see the nourishment that God provides for our tummies as a blessing, He also provides nourishment for our souls through church, Bible studies, worship, and more. Where are you getting your spiritual nourishment? Be sure you are getting fed in places that are God-centered and focused on His word.

30

Forbidden

I first noticed that the opposite sex was something to be admired when I was in kindergarten. His name was Nick, and he was so cute. He didn't speak to me, and I didn't speak to him, but I just knew he had to be mine. Whatever that means when you're six years old. He never became mine. We never even became friends. But for a few years, I was completely and utterly "in love" with Nick, the cute boy in my class.

Each year of school I liked a different boy, and the boy would never like me back. It wasn't that boys didn't like me, there were plenty of nerdy guys who wrote me the, "Will you go with me? Circle yes or no," letters. The answer was always no. I wasn't popular enough for the guys I actually liked to like me back. They were popular, and I was not.

In junior high, things changed. I certainly didn't become popular, but I started to notice guys who weren't popular, and I started having boyfriends. There was Ben, Andy, another Ben, Jason, and yes, another Ben. I don't know what it was about the name Ben, but there were a lot of mothers in Celina, Ohio who chose that name for their baby boys in 1980 and 1981.

In high school I dated, but nothing ever got serious. I spent most of high school obsessed with my two best friends: Brett and

Greg. I'd go back and forth in my heart as to who was my best friend and who was the love of my life. To this day, I'm not sure which was which, but since I didn't end up with either of them, clearly, neither was the love of my life.

College was a train wreck when it came to my love life. I fell fast and hard for any guy with big brown eyes and a sultry smile. There were lots of those at Indiana University, and each one who stole my heart ended up shattering it to pieces.

I share all of that to say this: from a young age, I have appreciated the magnificent creature known as a "guy." I think that the male species is the most beautiful living creature that God created. And in Uganda, with one specific living creature, that was a problem.

The moment I saw him I was taken aback. I grabbed the arm of a friend and said, "Who is that?"

She laughed and told me who he was and then said, "You aren't the first. You won't be the last to notice."

He was one of the most gorgeous guys I had ever seen. However, he was totally off-limits for a variety of reasons.

One evening I was out to dinner with a friend who brought him up. Since she brought up how attractive he was, I felt comfortable telling her that I had a bit of a crush on him, no matter how forbidden it was.

"Oh, if anyone has a chance, it's you," she said.

"What?!" I nearly knocked over my bottle of Stoney. "Don't say that!"

"It's true," she said. "And I would fully support it. I mean, I know it would be wrong and all, but who could blame you?"

Not what I needed to hear. I wanted to be chastised for my feelings, not encouraged.

I even talked about it with a friend, the school's counselor, who I knew would squash whatever feelings I had.

"He is SO good-looking," she said. "It's OK to look. Just don't let anything happen. And I know you, it won't."

And it didn't. Nothing even came close to happening, but I did carry around the secret of my attraction to him like a sack of rocks on my shoulders. As I got to know him more, I got to see what an incredible person he was. Not only was he strikingly gorgeous, but he had an incredible heart. I thought about him every single day. It actually ended up being one of the reasons I decided not to return to Uganda for a second year.

CLOUDY BLESSING: Conviction

My secret never came to light with those around me, with the exception of a few who knew, but it was always in the light with God. It took me years after I'd returned from Uganda to face up to those feelings and ask for God to forgive me. Even though nothing ever happened, my thoughts were a sin.

"If we confess our sins, He is faithful and just and will forgive us our sins and purify us from all unrighteousness." 1 John 1:9

How blessed are we that God forgives us? No matter how awful the sin, no matter how dirty the secret, He will always forgive us. The price for our sins was paid when Jesus died on the cross. There is no greater love than that.

I can't imagine carrying my secret around the rest of my life and not asking for forgiveness. I also can't imagine how awful the burden would have been if something had happened with "him." I am so grateful to the Lord for not ever letting that be an option.

Although the secret was heavy for a long time, I can look back and see that the Lord was so, so good to me. Conviction kept me from making any mistakes I would later regret.

The Holy Spirit will let you know when you're doing something wrong. It's a sure-fire way to know you need to make a change. Then, no matter how dark the secret or how inappropriate the thought, God will forgive you if you ask. Take it all to Him, and He will make you clean, removing every cloud of sin from your heart.

31

Christmastime in Uganda

Christmas has always been one of my favorite holidays. It's not about the gifts. I love the excitement that lurks around every corner all December (and sometimes November) in every town in America. There are decorations and lights, and Christmas music fills the air. It would be next to impossible to deny the fact that it's Christmas time in America in the days leading up to December 25.

In Uganda, things were quite different.

Christmas was nearly a week away when I realized how unchanged things were around our apartment and Kampala as a whole. I noticed a little boy with a small homemade broom sweeping the dirt in front of his tiny home across the street from us. His mother was hanging lots of colorful laundry on the line, and his father appeared to be mashing something up for lunch. There were no Christmas lights or even a wreath on the door.

The intense Ugandan sun beat down on the tin roofs of the shacks behind our apartment. The beautiful, towering palm trees were a stark contrast to the dirty, rickety homes surrounded by chickens and naked children.

I could hear birds- lots and lots of different birds who sang their songs from the treetops where they no doubt had the best view of Lake Victoria and the rest of Kampala. A rooster crowed, and someone turned on their radio. A local radio host gave the morning news report in Luganda. The sound of it was temporarily interrupted by a big truck driving by, carrying policemen in the back who proudly held their rifles up as if to say, "Don't mess with us."

Our day guard sat under his favorite tree, wearing the same t-shirt and pants he had worn for the past few weeks. My American friend's little boy approached him with a stuffed SpongeBob and handed it to him. The guard, who appeared to be only about 15, just kind of looked at it and handed it back. He spoke no English, so we knew absolutely nothing about him... except that he liked to climb trees.

I got a whiff of the familiar nauseating smell that so often permeated the area around our apartment. From our second-story balcony I could see piles of trash in the nearby field. Chickens and goats rummaged through the piles looking for something to eat, and a handful of Ugandan children played soccer, dodging the hordes of garbage people had dropped off in the field.

It was hot. It was smelly. It was dirty. It was beautiful. It was Uganda. And it was Christmastime.

You would never know it.

Sure, inside our apartment we had nativity scenes, a small Christmas tree, and even stockings hung. But other than that, it was life as usual for most people.

I won't go off on the whole, "Christmas isn't about all that commercial stuff anyway" tangent that so many people seem to enjoy. While that's true, I don't think God has any problems with decorations and festivities that celebrate Jesus' birth. And I'm not going to pretend that I didn't miss all of that the year I spent Christmas in Uganda. For me, it's always been a big part of what makes Christmas special.

Knowing that the approaching holiday would be unlike any we'd experienced in the past back in the U.S. with our families, we decided to make it as special as possible. On Christmas Eve we went swimming, and I even wore my Santa hat in the swimming pool. That evening we went to a candlelight worship service with faculty and staff from school.

On Christmas morning, I woke up and eagerly went out to our little Christmas tree where one gift waited for me. It was a box my parents had sent me. It came in the mail a few days before, but I made myself wait so I would have something to open on Christmas day. I was elated to find my favorite chocolates inside, some new shirts and leggings, a new Tervis cup, and other goodies stuffed inside the box. It was the best gift ever. The best part of the gift were two letters, one from my mom and one from my dad. Every Christmas we write each other letters and read them before we open gifts. Although a world away, we weren't going to let that tradition die.

Amanda and I got dressed and went downstairs to see our good friend, Nawanda, and her sons. The boys had already opened their gifts and were running around playing. We made ourselves a delicious breakfast and enjoyed each other's company until we went for Christmas dinner at a friend's house. It was definitely an unforgettable Christmas.

For 32 years I'd spent Christmas day with my mom and dad, and this was the first year that I didn't. However, I believe it was also the first year that I was exactly where God wanted me to be. I felt blessed, thankful, and humbled by my experience in Uganda. I was thankful for a Savior who loved me enough to send me there.

CLOUDY BLESSING: Baby Jesus

For some reason, God didn't want me around the glitz and glam of an American Christmas in 2013. For years I had great expectations of Christmas, but nothing could prepare me for a Christmas abroad. It was quiet and peaceful, but still a celebration for the birth of our Savior.

"The shepherds returned, glorifying and praising God for all the things they had heard and seen..." Luke 2:20

Sure, we see Jesus as a blessing, but what about Baby Jesus? What about the fact that Jesus came to us as a baby and went on to save the world? That is certainly something worth celebrating! The fanfare of an American Christmas is lovely, but it doesn't matter where you are when it comes to celebrating the birth of Jesus. The birth of our Savior should be celebrated every single day.

32

Ringing in 2014

It was New Year's Eve, and we wanted to do something fun to ring in 2014. However, many people let us know that being outside and anywhere near downtown Kampala after dark on New Year's Eve would be dangerous. The year prior, a teacher attended the downtown festivities and was punched by a random person for no reason. A few others had been mugged. So, we knew we had to have our fun in the daylight and ring in the new year that night back in the safety of our apartment.

"Ready?" Sasha asked. Sasha and her husband Tim lived in the apartment below us. They had lived in Uganda for a few years and were very acclimated to everything Uganda. They even had a nice big car that we would all fit into for excursions, and on this New Year's Eve day, we were headed to Jinja.

It takes an hour or two to travel to Jinja, depending on traffic, and once we arrived, I instantly fell in love. Jinja was a small town, nothing like Kampala. It had a very serene and chill vibe and was located on the shores of the Nile.

"There are two things you need to know about where we're eating lunch," Sasha told us as we parked the car. "One, they have fancy coffee drinks. Two..." she paused for effect, "they have ranch dressing."

Amanda and I shrieked with joy. None of the restaurants we went to in Kampala had ranch dressing. Some didn't even know what it was.

I ordered a vanilla latte that arrived with "Happy New Year" written in the foam, and a sandwich with French fries. And yes, I dipped my fries in ranch, and it was delicious. I would say that was the highlight of our day, but there was much more excitement just around the corner.

Sasha and Tim took us to a resort where we could take a boat and explore the Nile. We hopped into the Jesus Boat and were treated to an incredible Nile River boat ride. We saw monkeys, fish, birds, and crazy-looking reptiles all in their natural habitat. This wasn't a ride at a theme park, this was the real deal. I kept thinking about how we were in the very river mentioned in the Bible in so many great stories, and it gave me chills.

My chills weren't over when we left Jinja. We stopped at a petrol station to fill up on the way home, and Amanda and I went inside to grab some snacks. There it was. It was as if the heavens had parted and the sun illuminated what stood before us: Dr Pepper. It was a very, very rare find at the time. Not even the U.S. Embassy supermarket sold Dr Pepper. Clearly I had to splurge, and I paid around $5 for a single can of Dr Pepper.

"I'm going to drink mine at midnight to ring in the new year!" I told everyone. Then, I took a selfie with my can of Dr Pepper to share the experience with my friends and family back in America.

But drinking my Dr Pepper at midnight didn't happen. We got back to the apartment at around 7 p.m. and decided to play some card games while we waited for it to be midnight. By around 10 p.m., we were done, exhausted from the day's festivities. My Dr Pepper would have to wait. I crawled into bed and fell asleep before 11.

BAM! BAM! BOOM! CRACK! POW POW!

I woke up with a jump. I knew it must be midnight. Not only were fireworks exploding everywhere, but people were shooting their rifles and other firearms into the air. The scene gave me an eerie feeling, but I was happy to be safe and sound inside our apartment.

God, I prayed, please keep everyone safe tonight. Thank you for keeping me safe.

Once the commotion settled down, I went back to sleep.

CLOUDY BLESSING: Memories

New Year's Day was the treat I envisioned, simply because I was able to have my Dr Pepper. I savored it at lunch with high hopes that 2014 would be an amazing year, whether I stayed in Uganda or returned home. The decision would weigh heavily on my heart in the weeks that followed, but I made sure to draw close to God so I would know what to do when the time came.

At the time, I was so broken that I didn't fully realize it, but I was experiencing so many unforgettable memories. Although I was fighting a deep depression, God was blessing me with memories to last a lifetime. I will always remember my New Years in Uganda. What memories are you thankful for? Be sure to thank the God that gave you such incredible memories!

33

The Smallest Details

I was in paradise. I thought I'd seen paradise before in the Caribbean, or even on the shores of Nicaragua. But the shores of the Indian Ocean in Mombasa, Kenya... this was paradise.

I had my own room on the bottom floor of what could only be described as a luxurious hut. Just a few steps away was a path to the breakfast area, past towering palm trees and the occasional monkey and beautiful, exotic birds. I was delighted to experience another morning of gluttonous breakfast food at my disposal on the buffet. I ate a mango, an omelet, bacon, and coffee with sugar and cream while overlooking the Indian Ocean. I could see all kinds of boats and people. I watched big boats carrying cargo, as well as small fishing boats that were scattered about the horizon, which made the ocean look like it went on forever. There were even some men walking camels along the beach, the tan hair of the camels a stark contrast to the bright blue water. The ocean breeze tousled my hair and tickled my nose. I smiled and took in everything around me. I was in heaven.

I finished my glorious breakfast at the café and decided to go for a walk on the beach. The sun was beaming down on me, and the cool water of the Indian Ocean was sweeping over my tanned feet. The shallow water I waded through was crystal clear, not even blue or turquoise. Naturally, I was taking hundreds of photos of the utopia that surrounded me. These would make some seriously amazing Instagram posts.

"Jambo!" I heard a voice say behind me.

I turned around to see a thin young man with dreadlocks smiling at me. He wore a lot of jewelry made out of shells and beads, and he carried a small backpack with the Jamaican flag on it. My friend Melinda would love him, as his hair and style were definitely her "type" but not mine at all.

"Hi!" I said to him. He looked to be in his early 20's and had a smile as wide as the ocean seemed deep.

"I am Captain Samson," he said in his beautiful Kenyan accent and extended his hand. "Let me show you some of the things on the shore you are missing."

He seemed nice enough. The beach wasn't super populated, but enough so that I didn't think he could kidnap me or anything without anyone noticing. This only entered my mind because of the warnings we had been given about being too trusting of strangers when in new areas.

"I have a boat, you come with me," he said.

I stopped in my tracks. Maybe I was wrong.

"Oh, no thank you," I said. "I am not supposed to leave."

"Then we will walk," he said.

Captain Samson and I walked along the beach for hours. He knew everything there was to know about the creatures of the Indian Ocean. It didn't take long for him to find a couple of starfish. One was red and pink, and the other was yellow and orange. They were the most beautiful starfish I'd ever seen, much different than the ones I'd seen in the Gulf of Mexico.

"I will take your picture," he said as I handed him my camera, and he placed a starfish in each of my hands. They were so vibrant and beautiful. They almost seemed like synthetic works of art that an earthly artist had created in a studio, when in actuality they were created by the ultimate artist, God. In some parts, the starfish felt rough and bumpy, and in others, they were smooth as could be. Captain Samson returned the starfish to the water and motioned for me to follow him through the perfectly clear, shallow water.

A few yards later, he scooped up a small sea urchin and tried to place it in my hand. I jumped back, but he assured me it was safe. I was hesitant, but I allowed him to place the foreign animal in my open palm. It had long spikes and barely moved, but if you looked close enough and held really still, you could see it moving ever so slowly.

"It will move slowly, slowly," he explained.

Then he flipped it over and showed me the mouth and explained how it eats. Its prickly exterior began to tickle my hand, and I laughed.

"Hakuna matata!" he said with a laugh as he returned the sea urchin to its home in the ocean.

Captain Samson showed me many more living creatures around the shore and in the water. He explained in great detail how the creatures move, eat, and defend themselves. We came across a large sea urchin, close to the size of a bowling ball. Captain Samson told me that we couldn't touch the larger ones because they would sting us.

I was in Kenya for our mission's annual retreat, and at one of our prayer meetings, we read Psalm 139 "The All-Knowing, Ever-Present God." It talked about how God knows everything we do and think, even before we do it or think it. God knows all the details of our lives.

Learning about the sea creatures reminded me that God orchestrated everything. He even took the time to perfectly create the creatures of the sea, each and every detail of their existence. If God took that much pride in creating sea creatures, think of how much He cares about the details of our lives. We are His most prized and special creations.

CLOUDY BLESSING: Uniqueness

"For it was You (God) who created my inward parts; You knit me together in my mother's womb. I will praise You, because I have been remarkably and wonderfully made." Psalm 139: 13-14

The paradise in Mombasa was a stunning reminder of some of the most beautiful things God put on this planet. The details in the seashells, monkeys on the shore, and towering baobab trees were made perfect by Him.

If God took the time to care about the intricate details of sea creatures and other living things around us, just think of the amazing care and detail He put into planning your life, which is uniquely yours! Be sure to thank Him for making you just the way you are. Don't cloud your vision with expectations of what the world wants you to be. You are uniquely created by a heavenly Father.

34

A Sabbath Rest

I love a good motivational speaker. They can get me pumped up to read my Bible, to lose weight, to manage my time better, or to use essential oils for every ailment. A great motivational speaker can get you excited about nearly anything. They present material in ways we've never heard before. Their words make us laugh, and they make us cry. They are professionals at what they do, and often, God is using them to minister to the rest of us and change our lives by leading us to Him.

God used a few motivational speakers to change my life in 2012. An older friend from a Bible study group invited me to attend "Fresh Grounded Faith" with her at a local church. It had been a long time since I had attended any sort of Christian conference, so I figured the event would be good for me. It was November, and I had no idea that God would be sending me to Uganda in eight months. God used Jennifer Rothschild and Lisa Welchel to stir my soul that weekend. I was uplifted, convicted, and reminded of why we are so blessed to serve such an incredible God. I look back at that weekend as one of the major turning points in my life. We even memorized a verse that I still repeat each night before I go to bed:

"Because of God's great love, we are not consumed. His mercies are new every morning. Great is His faithfulness. Therefore, I will say to my soul, the Lord is my portion, and I will trust in Him." Lamentations 3:22-24

Fast forward to a little more than a year later, and there I was in Mombasa, Kenya for our World Missions Organization retreat. Each year they hired a speaker to lead the WMO missionaries through the retreat. That specific year, we had the most amazing motivational speaker. You could definitely say the best in the world. Our speaker was God.

It was different. It wasn't the typical retreat, but it was exactly what I needed at the time.

"Sabbath by the Sea" was the theme, and it was all about spending one-on-one time with God in whatever way each person needed. We met in the morning for a brief prayer meeting and then again in the evening. Other than that, the time was between me and God. I talked to Him by the pool and as I walked along the stunning shores of the Indian Ocean. There's something both special and surreal about not only talking to God but just listening.

On that first day in Mombasa, I wrote the following prayer in my journal:

Dear God, Your creation is so beautiful. Only someone of your perfection could create this gorgeous place. I watch the contrast of the sinful people on the beach with your flawless ocean and sand. I am one of those people. We all are, and yet you allow us, and even welcome us, to experience your beauty here on the beach. Thank you, God, for the beauty of this earth. Sometimes all we dwell on is the ugly, but everything You made is good. We must spend more time realizing that. In these next few days, I will notice the good and the perfection of Your work, and I will listen to what You have to tell me.

The next day, I took note of what God had to tell me.

As I soak up the sun's rays beside the pool, I am reminded that today we are to receive. I receive the intense sunlight as I also receive what You want to tell me. Am I to keep it a secret, the powerful wisdom and comforting peace you want me to receive? Of course not! Like the sunlight reflects off the water, You want me to reflect you in everything I do. I am blessed to serve a God who wants me to not only give to Him, but to also receive from Him. There is no greater joy than serving my King and receiving the blessings He has for me.

Between the prayer meetings and my quiet time with God, I learned a lot about the "Sabbath" and how powerful it can be. The dictionary defines the Sabbath as "a weekly day of rest or time of worship." For Christians today, this day is on Sunday. But Sabbath doesn't just have to be on Sunday. And it doesn't have to be about going to church.

"There remains, then, a Sabbath-rest for the people of God; for those who enter God's rest also rest from their own work, just as God did from His. Let us, therefore, make every effort to enter that rest." Hebrews 4:9-11

Make every effort to rest? Easier said than done. There's so much to do. Even in Uganda, away from our first-world responsibilities, there was so much to do. There was lesson planning, grading papers, youth group, meetings, volunteering, grocery shopping, and more. When in the world was I supposed to rest?

Western culture tells us to be busy. It tells us to be as busy as we possibly can, and sometimes it even feels like a contest to see who is the busiest. Rest is almost frowned upon by our society. It's often seen as lazy. Then, we are reminded that even God rested! He set the ultimate example of rest for all of us when He created the earth.

CLOUDY BLESSING: Sabbath Rest

"By the seventh day God had finished the work He had been doing; so on the seventh day He rested from all His work." Genesis 2:2

And WE are too busy to rest? What a ridiculous thought.

I learned so much on that restful retreat in Mombasa. I learned how to rest and that God commands us to do so. He even exemplified the behavior for us.

"Where can I go from your Spirit? Where can I flee from your presence? If I go up to the heavens, you are there; if I make my bed in the depths, you are there. If I rise on the wings of the dawn, if I settle on the far side of the sea, even there your hand will guide me, your right hand will hold me fast." Psalm 139:7-10

Are you taking the time to rest as God did? You don't have to be "by the Sea" or anywhere special. You can have a restful and inspirational Sabbath no matter where you are because God is always there, too. If you must, put a time to rest on your calendar or set an alarm on your phone. There is so much good that God can do for us if we simply rest.

35

An Evening with Jean-Claude

There was one constant that brought me joy throughout my time in Uganda: food. I didn't gain weight (I actually lost some) because of all the walking we did and a lack of processed food, but just as it did back in the U.S., food brought me joy. So, when a friend whose husband worked with Samaritan's Purse invited me over for a special dinner, I didn't hesitate to say, "Yes!"

There were around six of us, and our friend Kelly said there would be a special guest cooking our meal. His name was Jean-Claude Mille, and he was a big deal. We had no idea how big of a deal he really was until dinner was served.

Jean-Claude introduced himself in a thick French accent and explained the evening's menu: beef stroganoff for the main course and cream-filled crepes with mango sauce for dessert. He told us a little bit about what he does. He explained how he traveled the world to cook for missionaries and that he uses only local food to create unforgettable dinners.

Once dinner was ready, he brought out the main course and prayed over the food. Beef stroganoff might not sound impressive, but this dish, made by a world-famous chef, was out-of-this-world. It was one of those moments where you take a bite and have to close your eyes to block out any distractions because it's just that magnificent. You want to savor every bite.

We laughed for a while, as Jean-Claude had all sorts of funny stories to tell us, before he dived into his testimony. "I do this because I love the Lord and the Lord has been good to me," he said. "But I have not always known the Lord."

Jean-Claude moved to the United States when he was 22 and found worldly success as a chef. He had often been requested by the members of the Rat Pack, like Frank Sinatra and Dean Martin. They had insisted on meals from Jean-Claude when in New York City, even in the middle of the night. But fame and impressive Hollywood connections led Jean-Claude into a life of drugs, and by the time he was 50, he couldn't hold down a job, and he became homeless.

With life just too much to bear, Jean-Claude planned to take his own life but heard from God in the nick of time. In 1995, Jean-Claude accepted Christ, and his life was forever changed. For seven years, beginning in 1995, he was the executive chef for The Billy Graham Training Center at The Cove. After that, he began traveling the globe to cook for veterans, missionaries, and those impacted by natural disasters. He spoke with such passion about all that God had used him to do. It was so clear that he had a heart for the Lord.

"And now," he said. "We enjoy dessert."

The mango crepes were unlike anything I'd ever tasted. The flaky crepes and the smooth, creamy filling were a perfect match with the sweet mango sauce that was spooned on top.

I selfishly wanted to hear more about Frank Sinatra and Jean-Claude's days cooking for the rich and famous in New York City, but those days were not the highlight of his chef career or his life.

His highlight was what he was doing for us: cooking us a delicious meal and sharing his testimony.

CLOUDY BLESSING: Hope

"And though your beginning was small, your latter days will be very great." Job 8:7

That verse from Job made me think of Jean-Claude, how his beginning, although big to the world around him, was actually so small. His great days were ahead of him. Perhaps he wasn't famous anymore, perhaps he wasn't wining and dining with celebrities, but he was working for the Lord, and there was nothing greater than that.

I could relate. I had a past of partying and looking for contentment in everything except the Lord. My beginning was small. And although living in Uganda for a year was the struggle of my life, my latter days were very great, indeed.

I was on a mission trip in Thailand in 2015 when I heard that Jean-Claude had passed away. It was one of the top news stories around the world, celebrating his life and all the wonderful things he had done. I pray I have even half the impact he had on so many lives for Jesus.

It's never too late to make a change in your life and live it the right way. God will do big things in your life if you turn the reins over to Him. He is our only hope. Like Jean-Claude, we should be telling everyone about the wonderful hope found in Jesus Christ.

36

Insecurity or Selfishness?

When I was living in Uganda, smack-dab in the middle of God's will for my life, I expected my insecurities to melt away. How on earth, I wondered, could I be insecure when I was doing exactly what God wanted me to do? It was one of many misconceptions I had before moving to Uganda.

Insecurity was something I'd always battled. Although I had wanted nothing more than to be popular back in elementary school, I was far from it. The popular kids usually made fun of me. Then, in high school, my family moved, and somehow, I was popular at my new school. However, my insecurities only increased. There was a lot of keeping up in being popular. There were a lot of rules to follow, and I worried that one day I would screw up and lose my place among the popular crowd.

But when I moved to Uganda to do what God wanted me to do, I was sure that my insecurities would melt away. As it turns out, my insecurities became magnified overseas, and it took a selfish thought at a little boy's birthday party to make me realize how ridiculous my insecurities were and how Satan was the one throwing them in my face.

It was a Sunday afternoon, and a bunch of teachers and their families gathered in the Redemption cafeteria for the birthday party of a teacher's son.

Rebecca, the wife of our music teacher at the school, got to the party late. You could spot her beautiful smile and long blonde hair from across the campus as she neared the party with her husband by her side. On this particular day, she was carrying an African baby.

Teachers rushed towards her.

"We had to bring Ryan with us," she said. "He just got out of the hospital, and we couldn't let him go back to that baby home. He needs better care."

Everyone at school knew and loved baby Ryan. Ryan had AIDS and was living in a baby home for orphans in Kampala. Many of us had volunteered there, and we knew it was no place for a baby to recover from a hospital stay, especially a baby who was so sick. What Rebecca and her husband were doing was a really noble and beautiful thing. Poor baby Ryan DID need better care, and Rebecca and her husband could provide that. God was using them to do something selfless and admirable.

However, I didn't see that right away.

Why don't you have a baby, Natalie? I heard in my head. *I bet everyone here is wondering why YOU didn't go get baby Ryan at the hospital and bring him home with you. You haven't brought home any orphans to your apartment. Don't you care about the orphans, Natalie?*

I know, I know. It sounds ridiculous. No one was thinking that, but I feared they were. In my head, I made the entire situation about me. I couldn't believe that I didn't think to go visit Ryan in the hospital. I started to beat myself up in my head for not thinking of it. My thoughts snowballed as I wondered why I couldn't be like Rebecca, who was so perfect. I knew people didn't look at me like they did Rebecca, and I figured they were ashamed of me for not bringing babies home from the hospital, even though Rebecca was literally the only one who had done so.

Then, it was like God audibly sighed, and I was knocked back into reality. My thoughts were selfish. They were terrible. I had a habit of thinking that people thought about me way more than they possibly did.

CLOUDY BLESSING: Humility

"Do nothing out of selfish ambition or vain conceit. Rather, in humility, value others above yourselves." Philippians 2:3

Sometimes, selfishness is disguised as insecurity. We think that we're simply thinking poorly of ourselves, when actually, we're wanting more attention. We actually think we're pretty great, and we're annoyed that people aren't noticing.

The key is to start valuing others above ourselves. It's not a contest to see who can do the most good. I should have been overjoyed that baby Ryan had a loving couple that would take care of him as he recovered. Instead, I let my selfishness make it about me.

There's room for all of us to be good in this world, and it's not about everyone seeing how "good" you are. Follow what God wants you to do, and you'll be a shining light for HIM, not YOU. If there's an area of your life where you need a little more humility, try lifting someone else up. We're all in this together.

37

Car Accident: Part I

Pizza. We needed pizza. It had been a long day at school, and my roommate, Amanda, our neighbor, Nawanda, and her young son, and I needed pizza. We piled into my Toyota RAV 4 and headed for Uchumi market. There was a little pizza café in Uchumi, and our mouths were watering as we headed there.

But getting to Uchumi meant driving on Gabba Road. Gabba Road, like most roads in Kampala, was a traffic nightmare. There were people everywhere and so many bodas every which way you looked, weaving in and out of traffic.

As I approached Uchumi on my right (driving on the left side of the road as they do in Uganda), I was surprised to look around and see no one coming from either direction. This was a very rare site on Gabba Road, and I felt blessed that my right turn into the Uchumi parking lot from the left lane was going to be an easy one. Just as I turned, a boda appeared out of nowhere and tried to pass me on the right. The boda crashed into my car with a thud. The boda, its driver, and the passenger tumbled into a pile on the side of the road.

To help you visualize this as an American driver, imagine turning left into a parking lot and someone decides to whiz up on you and pass you on the left. Totally illegal.

Illegal in Uganda? Who knows. That was the last thing on my mind at the time. All I could remember was that I had been told: if you are ever in an accident in Kampala, do NOT stop. Do NOT get out of your vehicle. Drive to a police station. The issue was, as Americans, there's something that feels very wrong about leaving the scene of an accident. I just couldn't do it, especially when I realized the boda passenger was injured.

I pulled off to the side of the road. It didn't take long for a crowd to form. We got out of the car as the angry boda driver and passenger approached us.

"Why did you hit me?" the driver yelled.

"Actually, you hit me!" I blurted out. "I was turning right, and you passed me on the right! You can't do that, sebo!"

The crowd continued to grow and surround my car. I began to remember why we were taught to leave the scene of an accident: mobs. Angry mobs of people will form and danger will ensue. The passenger from the boda was bleeding badly from his leg.

"Madame, get back in your car!" an elderly Ugandan man, who I now believe was an angel, said as he grabbed my arm. "They will set your car on fire. You have to leave."

"But it wasn't my fault!" I said, trying to keep calm. "Anyone around could have seen that it wasn't my fault!"

"That doesn't matter, Madame," he warned. "Please, I beg of you, get back in your car! They will hurt you!"

My friends and I jumped back into the car as the crowd continued to grow with each passing minute. I had no clue what to do.

The crowd was so large that I couldn't even move my car without running people over. I rolled my window down and said to the boda driver, "I am going to call the police." Not that I knew how. Uganda doesn't exactly have 911.

"No, no, no," he said. "There is no need to involve the police. Just pay me now."

I also knew that this was common, to settle disputes without the police. This also told me that he knew he was in the wrong. I refused to negotiate, and the crowd grew angry. They banged on our windows and rocked the car.

A local traffic cop made his way through the mob and spoke with the man who had warned us to get back into the car. The man said he saw the whole thing, and it was the boda driver's fault. The traffic cop then addressed the crowd, "He said it was the boda driver's fault."

The mob wasn't happy with that. Whether or not the man was telling the truth didn't matter, he was taking the side of a Mzungu. That was unacceptable.

The gentleman looked at me through the car window, a look of fear and panic in his eyes.

"I think he should get in with us," Nawanda said. "I think they might hurt him."

I asked if he wanted to get in the car with us, and he did. The traffic cop shrugged his shoulders and left. Apparently, worrying about the safety of a car full of Americans being mobbed wasn't important.

There we were: two white girls, our Sudanese friend and her young son, and a Ugandan man, who we eventually learned was a preacher, sitting in my Toyota, surrounded by an angry mob of people. I tried calling everyone I knew on my cell phone, but no one was picking up. My fear might not have been so bad if it weren't for the Ugandan man in our car telling us horror stories of what he'd seen mobs do to people before. He was horrified, and fearful the mob would either roll the car over or set it on fire with us still inside.

All of a sudden, we heard a horn and the crowd turned its attention somewhere else. It was a fellow Mzungu pulling up near the crowd. He got out of his car and shoved his way through the mob to reach my window. Another angel.

"Are you guys ok?" he said. He was an American. "I'm with the U.S. Embassy. I was driving by and saw the crowd. This is one of the biggest I've ever seen! What's going on?"

We quickly explained, and then he said to sit tight, and he would take care of it.

A few minutes later, a truck filled with the Ugandan version of a SWAT team showed up. There were about a dozen policemen with rifles in the back of the truck. That was what finally got the crowd to disperse. Then, we were able to leave and drive to a police station, where, to my surprise, the nightmare was far from over.

But at least the immediate danger was over. Two fellow missionaries from my organization met us there. When I saw them I burst into tears and sobbed for the first time that day. I was crying so hard I could barely breathe.

I have terrible anxiety. I take medication for it. I pray about it. I've been to counseling for it. Somehow, I held it together in the midst of that chaos. I know it wasn't my meds. It was possibly adrenaline, but who gave me the adrenaline to keep my calm during a horrifying situation? God did. He designed me that way. He designed all of us that way. We survive the scary moments because He lives within us.

CLOUDY BLESSING: Help

"The Lord is with me; I will not be afraid. What can man do to me? The Lord is with me; He is my helper." Psalm 118:6-7

Man can certainly hurt me physically. Christians are not immortal or somehow immune to being harmed physically, but man cannot take my soul or ruin my relationship with Christ. The Lord is with me, therefore whether it is on this earth or in heaven, He is with me.

"So do not fear, for I am with you; do not be dismayed, for I am your God. I will strengthen you and help you; I will uphold you with my righteous right hand." Isaiah 41:10

God is with you. He will give you the help you need to make it through whatever it is you are facing. A car accident in Africa, losing your job, losing a loved one, or, heaven forbid, losing multiple people you love all at once... He is still there. In the midst of your storm and trauma, He is there to clear away the clouds and be the help you need.

38

Car Accident: Part II

"Would you like a banana?" a woman asked as she poked her head into the office where we were sitting. She was carrying a large number of bananas on her head and was walking around the police station selling them.

"No thank you," I said. The couple from my organization who were with me also refused.

You know those movies where people go to jail in a foreign country? It's dirty, unorganized, and kind of scary? This particular police post was exactly like that. It may even have been a little worse. The cement walls and floors were dirty, the doors didn't close (some of them didn't even fit the doorways, they were about three inches too short and about three inches from the ground), and there were no lights in the hallways.

Also with us in the room was the Ugandan pastor who witnessed the accident, the boda driver, the boda passenger, and an officer.

The female officer sitting behind the desk took out a sheet of white paper and began to write in pencil. There wasn't a computer in sight. She asked the pastor, who served as a witness, something in Luganda, the local language, and he responded in Luganda.

Then the boda driver jumped up and started yelling something else in Luganda.

We had no idea what was going on.

The boda driver then yelled at the pastor, and a look of horror spread across the pastor's face.

"He has threatened my family," the pastor told us in English, "because I am saying the accident was his fault. He is saying he will come after my family."

The officer taking notes nodded her head in agreement like it was no big deal that this man and his family had just been threatened.

After some more discussion, we discovered that not only did the boda driver not have insurance, but he didn't even have a license.

We each gave our account of what happened, and then the officer put her pencil down. She took out a hole punch from a drawer and punched holes in the paper. Next, she took out a roll of yarn and tied it in the holes to make it into a booklet. Then, she threw it on a pile behind her on top of other booklets made the same way. It reminded me of books we used to make in elementary school.

"I am tired," she said. "We will finish tomorrow. Come back in the morning."

The next morning, we sat around for hours waiting to be seen by the officer in charge of our case. This time the boda driver brought his boss, the woman who runs the boda service he worked for.

As the officer reviewed our case, it seemed she was leaning in my favor.

"You don't have a license," she said to the driver. "You don't have insurance. You should be cited."

Then the man's boss said to the officer, "Let's take a walk," and the two of them left.

We knew what was happening. The woman was likely paying off the officer to protect her driver. This was apparent when they walked back in the room about an hour later, and the case was closed: I was cited for reckless driving. Everything was my fault, and I would pay the fine.

But it wasn't my fault. I had my first true, personal taste of injustice. It just wasn't fair, and there was nothing I could do about it.

CLOUDY BLESSING: Control

I cried a lot that week. I cried the night of the accident and after each visit to the police station (there ended up being about five total visits). I felt 100% defeated. Sometimes one incident can make it feel like everything has been ruined. I became certain that I never should have even gone to Uganda. I feared driving and getting into another accident that wouldn't be my fault, but I would be blamed for it.

Jesus's calming words in John 16:33 remind me how small my situation was. "I have told you these things, so that in me you may have peace. In this world you will have trouble. But take heart! I have overcome the world."

What I love about that verse is that Jesus didn't deny that we would have troubles. It is a certainty! But our troubles are insignificant in light of the fact that He has overcome the world.

It was OK that I was shaken by my experience, and it was traumatizing in so many ways. As it turned out, the man from the U.S. Embassy who stopped to help was the parent of a student at our school. I would later find out that he said it was one of the worst mobs he'd ever seen. We were very, very lucky we weren't harmed.

Even in the most tumultuous of situations, God is in control and can offer peace and comfort. We will have many troubles, but God is always in control, giving us the opportunity to turn the scariest of situations over to Him. Turn control over to God with whatever it is you are facing.

39

No Power, No Problem

Dinnertime for us was always interesting. On most nights, Amanda and I would cook our dinner and eat in our individual bedrooms in front of a laptop watching DVDs. My dinner of choice was almost always French fries or tuna salad. I would make the fries myself and dip them in mayonnaise. The tuna I would mix with mayonnaise. There was a lot of mayonnaise in my life when I lived in Uganda. (OK, so anyone who knows me well knows that this has always been the case and still is!)

Sometimes we would eat out, especially after a hard day. Café Roma was a popular, nearby Italian restaurant. We also liked a place called Paradiso, which had the best spaghetti carbonara I've ever had. Sometimes we would spring for Indian food and eat at the Coconut Shack or Khazana. If we felt like Mexican, we would head to The Little Donkey, where they served incredible guacamole.

was by far my favorite place. They had a cheese and tomato sandwich that I still crave every now and then. I always got a side of fries and mayonnaise, and drank either a Stoney or one of their to-die-for shakes. If I was feeling especially hungry, I'd cap the meal off with a slice of their delectable chocolate fudge cake. My mouth is watering as I think about it!

There was also the time my roommate and I decided to eat "raw" for a week. Just fruits and vegetables all week long. We went to the market and loaded up on amazing fresh produce. Our adventure lasted through one breakfast and one lunch. By dinner time we were over it, and we went to The Little Donkey for some Mexican food. I told you, that guac was irresistible.

And on special, rare occasions, we would cook dinner together with friends.

On one Thursday night in April, me and my roommate, Amanda, had Elizabeth, Sasha, and Nawanda and her two young sons over to make salad and mini pizzas. Just as we were about to start preparing dinner, the power went out.

"No!" we all screamed. The thing with a Ugandan power outage was that it could last for an hour. It could last for a day. It could last for a week, sometimes longer.

It was after 7 p.m., so it was already dark out. Power outages were common enough that we had a flashlight nearby. Amanda flipped it on to illuminate the room.

"What do we do?" she asked.

"Well, if the power is out for a long time, all of our ingredients are going to go bad," I said.

Sasha spoke up, "Guys, it's a gas stove. We can still make the pizzas and bake them, we'll just have to do it by candlelight!"

We grabbed all the candles we had to light up the kitchen, and we even turned on some 90's tunes on someone's laptop. Before we knew it, we were dancing around the kitchen, singing into paper towel rolls, cutting up vegetables for the salad, and putting toppings on our French bread mini pizzas. While we thought the power outage was going to ruin our evening, it ended up making for an evening we would never forget. It's one of my favorite

Ugandan memories with my friends, and we have the photos to prove it.

I've seen God work like that a lot. Something happens to upset me, like plans being canceled, and then something happens that's even greater. It can be so hard to trust that God has a plan, but He always does, and it's always what's best for us.

CLOUDY BLESSING: Perseverance

"You need to persevere so that when you have done the will of God, you will receive what He has promised." Hebrews 10:36

Don't give up when it feels like the lights have gone out or clouds appear to be ruining your day. Push through, and you might even find yourself better off than before.

40

Rock Bottom: Part I

There was a lot going on in my students' lives, things I didn't expect. What I really didn't expect was the way these things were handled by the school administration.

There was the boy on the basketball team whose anger issues began to scare some of his female classmates. They were legitimately worried he might hurt himself or someone else. I thought his mother, who was an administrator at the school, should know. I'm not sure if she ever addressed it with him, but I do know that she had it out for me after that, or so I was told by some other school employees. Things with her were never the same.

Things got worse later in the year when a student of mine confided in me that she had been cutting herself and was contemplating suicide. Back when I taught in the U.S. there were lots of students struggling with self-harm, and it was protocol to tell the school counselor, and they would take care of it from there. They would talk to the student and contact the parents. Our school was run like an American school, and we had the same rule: tell a counselor or the chaplain.

I told the chaplain, who then spoke with the woman in administration I mentioned above. She said I had to call the parents. I felt sick. I was certainly not qualified to discuss mental health issues of a child with this student's parents. To say that I flipped out would be an understatement. I remember standing in my room with the school chaplain and bursting into tears.

"I can't do that!" I yelled. "I don't know how to tell a parent that! I'm not qualified to do that! That's what a counselor does!"

"Well," she said, "that's what she says you have to do."

"Mandated reporting means I report it, that's it," I said. "I would have no idea how to instruct these parents to help her. I'm not trained in mental health issues. Wouldn't the school counselor be better off doing it?"

I was a mess. I cried and cried. I cried on my walk home. I cried in my bedroom. Even after the school counselor intervened and said she would call the parents, I was still a mess.

Then, I got to the point where I wasn't sure why my reaction was so strong, and it scared me. I was also really embarrassed. Really embarrassed. Embarrassment is something I have never handled well, and this was no different. I took it all in and began to tear myself apart.

You are a failure. I thought to myself. *You have made a mess of things, again. Why can't you just have normal reactions to situations? Why do you have to be so sensitive and overreact? What's wrong with you? You are worthless. No one here likes you. They probably want you to leave. Your student confided in you, and you don't even know how to help her. Why are you even here? Why are you even alive?*

It was a bottomless pit of self-degradation that I hadn't been down in many, many years. But there I was, falling hard and fast into the pit. I even felt like I was at the point of no return. I felt alone. I felt worthless. I wanted to die. I had never had such a strong urge to take my own life. There was an intense spiritual battle happening within me, and in that moment, I was letting Satan win.

When you're in the middle of severe depression, common sense is thrown out the door. You're so low that you think ending your own life would be the best route, that it would do everyone else a favor. While I obviously didn't end up taking it to that extreme, I did revert to something I hadn't done since college: I cut myself. I used this as a way of punishing myself for being so stupid, while also removing the focus from my emotional pain and turning it into physical pain.

The first time I cut myself was in high school. While it has unfortunately become a common practice for teen girls these days, back in the late 90s, no one was talking about cutting themselves. I hadn't read about it anywhere. I hadn't even heard of it. It was just something I started doing when I got really worked up and upset. I would use a safety pin or a thumbtack and cut my arms or legs until they bled. Not only did I not know anything about self-harm, but I knew little to nothing about depression and anxiety. It would be more than a decade before I learned that I was battling anxiety and depression. That's when I learned that therapy could help. That medication could help. And I also learned that both my mother and my grandmother faced the same issues with anxiety and depression. The women in our family just pass it on to the next generation.

But that day in Uganda, I was just done, more done than I had ever been in my entire life. Done with the façade of perfection for those back home, done with disappointing those around me, done with missing my family, and done with feeling like a failure. I sat on the floor of my bedroom, reached for a safety pin, and I cut myself on my arms. The scratches take a minute to appear, so I scratched deeper. Eventually, my arms were covered in red wounds. I was immediately ashamed. Immediately regretful. Immediately disappointed in myself. How childish of me!

At the time I didn't put two-and-two together. My reaction to talking to the student's parents was because I was exhibiting the same behavior as their teenage daughter. Cutting. Suicidal thoughts. There was no way I could have had that conversation with them when I was going through the same thing their daughter was. I couldn't offer solutions, because I didn't know any solutions. If I knew how not to self-harm, I wouldn't be doing it. But I knew I had to tell someone about what I was doing before it got worse. I told my roommate, the school counselor, and the school chaplain. They surrounded me with love and prayer. They even joined me on the floor in my bedroom.

"Do you need to go home?" the school chaplain asked me. "I don't think anyone would blame you if you went home."

"No," I said firmly. "Just hold me accountable. Check up on me. I promise I'll be fine."

I knew I was going to be OK, even if I still had three months left in Uganda.

While the next three months were tough, I didn't cut myself again. I knew that if I was going to counsel my students to not self-harm, I shouldn't be harming myself.

As far as the student who was cutting herself, we continued to develop a close bond, so much so that her parents took me out to lunch one Sunday afternoon after church. They were very thankful for the role I played in their daughter's life that year. It was the reassurance I needed to know that I was right where God wanted me to be, even if so much of it was painful.

CLOUDY BLESSING: Suffering

"For I consider that the sufferings of this present time are not worth comparing with the glory that is to be revealed to us." Romans 8:18

Even Christians aren't immune to anxiety and depression. We can fall just as low as anyone else if we let it take over our lives. Suffering might not seem like a blessing when we're in the middle of it, but when God reveals how He will use our suffering for His glory, we will see the blessing that it is.

41

Rock Bottom: Part II

What I didn't know about my depression and anxiety was that it would become a topic of gossip among some of my co-workers.

Let me back up. In January, when it was time to sign my teaching contract for my second year in Uganda, I struggled with what I was supposed to do. I'd said all along that God uses us wherever we are. I believed that whatever I decided about my future, it was ultimately between me and God. And that February I made the big decision – I would stay in Africa for a second year. I didn't feel God calling me to one specific place, and I believed He was leaving the choice up to me, that either way, He would use me. After all, "The Lord your God is with you wherever you go." Joshua 1:9

While I still felt that I couldn't go wrong with my choice, things changed. I started to feel uneasy, some things started to unravel, and my heart wasn't at peace. My health started getting worse. Some things were revealed to me that I never imagined would be revealed, including some things that my principal was saying about me.

I finally broke down one night while saying my prayers before bed, and I cried out to God:

God, I can't make this decision. I need you like I've never needed you before. I need you to make it clear. I need it to be crystal clear, spelled-out-in-the-sky clear. God, I am begging you. I need guidance and wisdom, and I need to know for sure what I am supposed to do.

The next day, God did just that. He revealed everything to me. He showed me things I hadn't seen before, and He made it clear, just like I had asked Him to.

"Answer my prayers, O Lord, for your unfailing love is wonderful." Psalm 69:16

It was that next day that I discovered not only my co-workers, but my administration had been gossiping about my mental health behind my back. I was called into the headmaster's office, and my friend, the Human Resources Director, came with me.

"Natalie, are you doing OK?" the Headmaster asked me in her thick British accent. "And by that, I mean, are you happy? Are you happy here?"

"At Redemption? I love it!" I said with complete honesty. I was happiest when I was at school with my students. School was my happy place.

"Well," she said. "I hear you've been unhappy, that maybe you're struggling with some depression? Some thoughts of hurting yourself?"

There was no reason for her to know this. The people who needed to know and could offer help already knew. The school counselor. The school chaplain. I felt like my privacy had been completely violated, and now I had to discuss it with a woman who had taken not one opportunity to get to know me the entire year. I knew others had horror stories about her, and I learned that this was now my time.

"I had a bad day," I told her. "I struggle with depression and anxiety, and this year has been really tough for me, but I love teaching at Redemption. I'm happy when I'm here at school."

She looked at me like I was a wounded puppy. "Are you sure you should come back next year?"

I figured that was my principal speaking through her. I knew she wanted me gone. This was my confirmation.

"Well, I don't know," I said. "This conversation, and knowing that my co-workers have been discussing me behind my back really makes me rethink things."

My friend said to the Headmaster, "Is Natalie in some sort of trouble? Has she done something wrong? It certainly seems like she's being reprimanded for something."

"No," the Headmaster said. "We're just worried about her."

It was odd that she claimed to care, given that neither she nor my principal checked up on any of us throughout the year to see how we were doing mentally. Not once was our mental health of concern to them.

She continued, "It just seems like this isn't the best place for Natalie."

I left the office a blubbering mess. Maybe she did care, but I was not in a place to see it at the time. I certainly felt like I was in trouble, and that didn't help my depression and anxiety. On my walk home, I remembered my prayer from the night before, the one where I begged God to tell me if I should stay another year or return home. It now seemed pretty obvious. I would go home at the end of the year and not return. There was no way I was coming back.

Some of my co-workers said I was just "under attack" from Satan, that he was the one who didn't want me to stay in Uganda, but as long as I walk this earth, and no matter WHERE I walk this earth, he will always be there looking to stop me from doing God's work. That would happen in America as well as Africa. I'd had enough conversations with God to know the difference, and I knew that He was closing the door on my time in Uganda.

My heart was broken. I wanted to come to Uganda and fall in love with life in Africa. I wanted to find my lifelong calling and serve God in Uganda for years and years, but what we want doesn't always line up with the plans God has for us. His plans, though, are always best.

The next day I met with the Headmaster again.

"Consider this my notice that I will not be returning next year," I said.

She looked shocked and upset. "Oh Natalie, I hate to hear that!"

"You pretty much made it sound like I had to leave," I told her.

"No, no!" she replied. "Not at all!"

My friend spoke up for me, "That's exactly what it sounded like." She was getting worked up, and I was so glad to have her there with me. "You were awful to her yesterday, and you made it very clear that she should leave. Don't backtrack and say you hate to hear that, when that's exactly what you said you wanted her to do."

"I'm sorry if I didn't express myself clearly yesterday," the Headmaster said, as if she had been speaking a completely different language and we misunderstood.

The entire situation was also one of the final straws for my friend, who had worked there for many years. She, too, would leave Uganda to the shock of everyone at the school.

CLOUDY BLESSING: Submission

I had to take a leap of faith before coming to Uganda, but to be honest, I felt like it was an even bigger leap of faith to go home. I would be unemployed, living with my parents, and trying to fit back into a society that was once normal to me but would seem so incredibly strange once I returned.

I had to be faithful that God would work it all out, and He gave me great peace with my decision.

"Submit to God, and you will have peace; then things will go well for you." Job 22:21

I would submit to God and leave Uganda.

When you're facing a decision, big or small, cry out to God and ask for guidance. His wisdom is infinite. Be faithful in prayer, and He will show you the way. Don't feel like you can't beg for His guidance. He will reveal what you need to know to make the right decision. Submit to Him.

42

The Happy Missionary

"Wow. Not exactly roughing it are you?" one of my supporters commented on a Facebook photo of the house I was staying in. I had never given the impression that I would be roughing it in Uganda. I made it clear that I'd be living in the capital city, in a home, with electricity and running water. I never once made it seem like I would be living in a hut in the middle of a primitive village.

It may have even appeared that I was not only not "roughing it," but living in paradise. There were palm trees, gorgeous sunsets, beautiful Lake Victoria, and we even had our own security guard. But the palm trees were dangerous when the branches and coconuts fell, Lake Victoria was filled with deadly bacteria and disease, and we had a security guard because, well, it was too risky to live without one.

On the outside, it might have appeared that everything was sunshine and rainbows. After all, it had to appear that way. Friends and family were paying for my time there with their financial support. I had to put on a happy face each and every day. When we did "rough it" on various trips and days without electricity, I felt like I had to talk about it so people knew I wasn't living in paradise.

With about a month left before heading back to Indiana, I started seeing a therapist for help with my depression and anxiety. I had experienced therapy before, back at home, for the same reasons. I'd battled depression and anxiety since college, and therapy always seemed to help.

"This is crazy," I said to the therapist. "I shouldn't be seeing you. Why am I such a mess here? I'm working for God, I'm following my calling! Missionaries don't come to therapy!"

She smiled. "Absolutely they do. Most of my patients are missionaries."

I was stunned. I remember thinking that couldn't possibly be correct. Why on earth would missionaries, besides myself, have to go to therapy? Even after nearly a year in Uganda that tore me to pieces, I was still convinced that everything should be perfect when you're serving the Lord. I felt that it was my fault that everything wasn't perfect for me. Clearly, I'd done something wrong.

She asked about the things I'd been through since coming to Uganda. I talked about spitting up blood every few weeks. I talked about the car accident, being mugged, missing home, the terror threats, and the lack of support from my principal.

"Do you realize the trauma you've experienced?" she said to me. "Moving across the world is stressful enough, let alone everything else you've been through this year. And the hardest part is, you probably feel like you have to pretend like everything is OK because people back home are supporting you financially."

Wow. She hit the nail on the head with that one. It was clear that I wasn't the first missionary to come to her with those exact feelings.

"I see a lot of missionaries," she continued. "Many of them struggle with depression, and it's made worse by this idea that they have to portray happiness all the time. When your friends and family are paying your bills and paying for your food, it's almost like you aren't allowed to ever be sad. You're doing God's work, so it's assumed everything is OK."

Everything was not OK, but I felt better knowing that other missionaries went through similar experiences. It felt better looking back at my year and realizing that, especially between my health issues and the car accident, I had experienced some trauma.

But, I felt like I had to play the part of the "Happy Missionary." I began to wonder about all the missionaries I knew around the world. Were they going through some of the same things I was going through but wearing a happy face through it all?

I learned that it was possible to trust God and still be sad. Trauma is tough to deal with, and it takes time to heal.

CLOUDY BLESSING: Restoration

Job is one of the greatest examples of trauma and devastation in the Bible. He had everything ripped away from him. At one point he asked God why he couldn't have died at birth. Job hated his life.

"I have no peace, no quietness, I have no rest, but only turmoil." Job 3:26

No peace. No quietness. No rest. Only turmoil. That is most certainly how I felt 90% of my time in Uganda. I wanted to love it. I wanted to be peaceful and happy, but those moments were so few and far between. But just like God restored Job by giving him twice as much as he had before, God would eventually restore me. He didn't let my depression in Uganda define me. He actually used it to refine me. It took years after coming home to see that, but I see it so clearly now.

"For you, O God, have tested us; You have refined us like silver." Psalm 66:10

God can, and will, refine you and restore you through trauma. The terrible times we survive are simply growing us, molding us into better humans for the glory of the Lord. Everything you have lost can be restored by the Lord.

43

Majestic Beauty Abounds

"Miss Trout, we want you to come with us on our senior trip," Dasha, one of my seniors, told me one day early in the year.

"Oh Dasha, that's really sweet," I said. "I'd love to, but your class sponsor is Mrs. Rogers. Usually your class sponsor goes with you."

"But we want you to go!" she exclaimed. "I speak for the entire class!"

I was flattered, especially to be chosen over Ashley Rogers, but she was also my friend, and I didn't want to hurt her feelings.

"Let me think about it," I told Dasha. I had to figure out how to approach this with Ashley, because not only did the students want me to go, but I really wanted to go with them.

Sometimes Ashley and I would take a walk around campus during our planning period, so I decided to bring it up then.

"Do the seniors know where they are going for their senior trip yet?" I asked her.

"Ugh," she sighed. "No, they have no idea. They've done a terrible job of fundraising, so they're pretty limited. They don't even want me to go, and I'm OK with that. They said they want you to go."

Wow. That was easy. She already knew.

"I don't know why they want me to go," I said. "I think you should go."

"Honestly, I usually want to go, but I haven't meshed well with this group. You have, Natalie, and you should go," Ashley said. "I think it would be great!"

No wonder Ashley was so well-liked and loved by everyone. She was seriously the best.

It was settled. I would go with the seniors on their senior trip.

When May rolled around, only seven of the ten seniors decided to join us. Jacob, the school music teacher, came along as the male chaperone.

It was a long drive to our destination, Katara Lodge, where we would be staying for four nights, but it was well worth the long trip. We got everyone checked in and were then shown to our rooms. As a single woman, I would have my own private space. I had no idea that at Katara Lodge, that meant I had an entire thatched cottage to myself.

I walked down the long walkway to my cottage and opened the door to a large room with open windows that overlooked the savannah, which was filled with grazing elephants. The view literally took my breath away. I had never seen such a beautiful sight. There was a small table and chairs in the room, as well as a sitting area with a couch and a chair. The big beautiful bed was surrounded by a mosquito net, of course. Next to the main bed was another bed, this one on wheels and next to the double doors that opened to the veranda, just in case you wanted to sleep under the stars.

I walked onto the veranda to get a better look at the view. For as far I could see, it was simply Africa, exactly as you would imagine it. Elephants, grasslands, a river, and hills all decorated the landscape while a bright blue sky with a beaming sun filled up the top half of my view. I felt like the view was infinite, like Africa just stretched out into forever. It brought me to tears. Few things have been so beautiful that they brought me to tears. One was Victoria Falls in Zambia, and the other was this sensational view from my very own cottage in the middle of Uganda.

The accommodations didn't stop there. I walked into the bathroom and gasped. There was a beautiful claw-foot bathtub and a rain shower that overlooked the savannah. I hadn't taken a bath in almost a year, and I'd been showering in the corner of our bathroom with a handheld showerhead that barely emitted a trickle of water. The bathroom alone in my cottage could have brought me to tears. There were also handmade soaps and lotions neatly placed on a hand towel next to the sink. I was in a Ugandan paradise.

I could have stayed in my cottage alone and into the night simply soaking in the breathtaking scenery, but we had a special drive to make through Queen Elizabeth National Park. We piled into two jeeps and headed out in hopes of finding some animals just before sunset. Unfortunately, our quest for animals fell short. We saw a few elephants and antelope, but no lions. However, it was still worth the ride to watch the sun set behind the Rwenzori Mountains. All year I had seen a graphic of the Rwenzori Mountains on the bottles of Rwenzori water I drank. Now, I was seeing them in person, their largeness creating majestic shadows in front of the colorful African sunset. I think I may have shed a tear at that view as well.

"Can you believe that, Miss Trout?" one of my students asked me. "How do you see that and not believe in God?"

He was right. There was no way science or the environment could create something so beautiful by chance. It was God's incredible artwork that we felt He'd arranged just for us that evening.

Our dinner back at the lodge was incredible, and then we retreated to our rooms fairly early because we had a big day ahead of us. Before bed, however, I couldn't pass up taking a luxurious bubble bath in my claw-foot bathtub. Then, I tucked myself into my massive, comfy bed and drifted off to sleep.

Pop pop pop. Pop pop pop. Pop pop pop.

I awoke with a startle at the sound sometime in the middle of the night. It was loud, and it was near. Then I could have sworn I heard an elephant. And a machine gun, maybe? I was glad I opted to sleep inside and not on the veranda. I pulled the sheet over my head and prayed everything was OK. Eventually, I fell back asleep.

The next morning at breakfast a few of the students were talking about the noise.

"I almost hid under the bed, man!" one said.

"You're such a wimp!" a female classmate joked with him.

"That is to scare away the elephants," our server told us. "The elephants try to get into the gardens at night, so the guards shoot their guns into the air to scare them away."

So, I was hearing guns and elephants after all. At least we knew what it was, but it was still unsettling. I decided I would not spend any nights out on the veranda. Sure, it would be a cool experience, but I was sure my anxiety would have gotten the best of me.

After breakfast, we headed out in our jeeps to look for lions. Sure enough, it didn't take long for us to run across six sleeping lions resting under some shade trees. They were magnificent. They looked so peaceful, like you could just walk up to them and pet them, maybe even lie down beside them. But these weren't trained animals. They weren't in a zoo or a rescue reserve. They were living their natural lives in their natural habitat. In the days that followed, we saw even more animals on our safari – crocodiles, elephants, hippopotamus, antelope, crested cranes, marabou storks, warthogs, bats, and even a python. It was overwhelming to see such magnificent creatures existing in the wild.

CLOUDY BLESSING: Creation

The ride home a few days later was a quiet one, as most of us slept. The parts of it I was awake, I was deep in thought. I had but a few days left in Uganda. I was overjoyed at the idea of going home, but I was also heartbroken at the idea of my experience ending. I knew I had some tough days ahead of me, but I thanked God for the adventure I had on the senior class trip. I saw God's awesome creations in a way I will never, ever forget.

"The heavens declare the glory of God; the skies proclaim the work of His hands." Psalm 19:1

Everything that is beautiful in this world is from God. Take a moment to soak it all in, and thank God for His magnificent creations.

44

Elephants on Safari

"He sees us!" I said as an enormous elephant nearby stopped what he was doing and made eye contact with us.

We did the natural next thing to do when an elephant spots you on safari. We took photos; lots and lots of photos. I was in awe of the big beautiful creature in the not-too-far distance. He was covered in wet mud, so I assumed he had just taken a nice mud bath and was eating breakfast. Although I'd seen many elephants on other African safaris, I never once stopped being mesmerized when I saw another one. They are magnificent, massive, beautiful creatures.

"Ready to move on?" our safari guide asked.

We agreed that we could move on. After all, on this particular day, we were hunting for lions. Finding lions is the most exciting part of a safari, but you are never guaranteed you'll find any. When I was on safari in Botswana, it didn't look like we would end up seeing any. Then, when we least expected it, watching from our boat in the Chobe River, we saw a lion attack a herd of cape buffalo. It was unexpected and glorious. It was like we were watching National Geographic, but it was happening right in front of our eyes. Once again, only this time in Uganda, I had high hopes of finding some lions, but as it turned out, finding lions wouldn't be the most adrenaline-filled moment of the day.

I was in a jeep with a safari guide and three of my senior students. The other jeep full of students was ahead of us. As we slowly began to drive through the rough terrain, the elephant we'd just been photographing kept his eyes on us and began to walk towards the path we'd been driving on.

"What's he doing?" one of my students asked, as the elephant walked onto the path behind us and stopped.

"No clue," I said. "But I don't like how he's looking at us."

Everyone in the jeep turned around to see what we were talking about. All of a sudden, the enormous elephant lifted his trunk. His ears flew out to his sides, making him appear even bigger than before. He shuffled his feet. And he began to charge towards us as we slowly drove away.

I don't know if you've ever been charged by an elephant (probably not), but know that A LOT goes through your mind in a short period of time. It's like being in a car accident. As the accident is happening, many images and ideas flow through your brain. That's what happened when that elephant started to run towards us. I envisioned us being trampled. I envisioned being the only one who survived. I thought I'd be left all alone with the elephant to fend for myself. And how in the world, I thought, would I explain to these students' parents that they were trampled by an elephant on the senior trip? What an ending to my year in Uganda that would have been! As if I wasn't insecure enough, now I didn't save my students from death by elephant.

As the elephant began to charge, one of my students shouted some words that good Christian boys should never say, but I couldn't blame him. I was thinking the same words as the deadly animal charged towards us. We were horrified. We were facing sudden death if this elephant continued to charge our jeep.

While we expected our driver to hit the gas and gun it forward, he did something none of us were prepared for. He stopped the jeep.

"GO! GO! GO!" we all screamed at our driver, thinking maybe he didn't realize what was happening. An elephant was charging at us in the middle of Uganda, and our driver stopped the jeep. At that moment, we feared it was the end. We were going to be trampled. But a few seconds after our driver stopped, the elephant stopped, and the driver revved the engine. Then, the elephant walked away in the opposite direction.

"You do not run when an elephant charges at you," our guide said in his thick Ugandan accent. "You stop, and they will go away. You do not want an elephant to chase you. You will lose."

He was correct. We did NOT want the elephant to chase us. We breathed a sigh of relief, my student apologized for his language, and we all had a good laugh. Everything was fine, and we weren't going to be trampled by an elephant.

Even though we knew all along that our guide knew what was best for the group and our safety, when it came time to really trust him, none of us did. We panicked. We said bad words. We feared for the worst.

CLOUDY BLESSING: Stillness

"Be still, and know that I am God." Psalm 46:10

Even when things aren't hectic, we can be still. Reading your Bible and praying are important, but sometimes we need to take the time to just sit and let the Holy Spirit move. Some of my greatest revelations about my life came when I was sitting quietly, asking God to speak to me.

I'm glad our guide knew to stop the jeep and not drive away. I'm also glad that in order to truly soak up what God has to say to me, all I need to do is be still and trust.

When things get scary, difficult, and even downright horrifying, we panic. We try to fix things. But just like our driver did when the elephant was charging at our jeep, sometimes we need to just be still. Let God be God.

45

Messages from the Heart

"I'm not like them." It was a common thought I had around big groups of Christian people with a certain personality and style of worship, and this was intensified ten-fold when I lived in Uganda. So many would raise their hands high and say, "Thank you Jesus!" throughout prayer and worship, while I would partially hold out my hands, close my eyes, and silently shed a few tears as I felt the Holy Spirit.

Others quoted scripture and often pulled it into their prayers when praying in front of everyone. I talk to God like He's my friend, and I suppose I don't quote scripture to Him because He already knows it.

After my thought of, "I'm not like them," often came the thought, "So I must not be as good of a Christian." You can see a pattern here from my time in Uganda- I never, ever felt good enough to be serving with the people I was serving with. They appeared to have been on the straight and narrow for far longer than I had. Many of them got married young and hadn't made the mistakes I had made. And Satan reminded me of this every single day. It was constant.

I knew better. I knew that God loved me just as much as He loves those who hadn't made big mistakes, and I knew that I didn't have to be like them to be a good person. I had to keep reminding myself that God had washed away my sins, and I needed to stop allowing Satan to get into my head and remind me of them. That certainly wasn't God doing that. So, each day I felt insecure or like I wasn't good enough to even call myself a Christian, I had to make the conscious effort to remind myself that I was. God loved me. He didn't make me with a personality to scream out to Him during prayer or worship. And that was OK.

But then a seriously disturbing thought hit me like a hurricane one day in Uganda: what if some of my students feel like I feel? What if I have students who look at some of the "super-spiritual" students and staff at school and think, "I'm not like that. I'll never be like that."

Conversations with my students ended up revealing that some of them did feel that way. They were never going to be so charismatic in their worship and praise, and it made some of them think, "Why bother?"

I knew I needed to say something. God told me I needed to say something. Yes, even though I'm not walking around quoting scripture and raising my hands in worship, I do talk to God. A lot. He gets me. And He knew it had to be said. So, one Friday afternoon in my classroom, I said it.

The main class I needed to say these things to were my seniors. They were an interesting bunch. Yes, I was teaching at a Christian school, but not all of our students were Christian. Many were simply "Christian" only because they had been forced to be. There were two boys who didn't even believe in God and had serious issues with Christianity and Christians in general. There was a Hindu girl and some students who had a strong faith in God but were not charismatic like a lot of their peers at school, and a few who actually were rather charismatic with their worship.

"So don't think that just because you're not loud and walking around campus quoting scripture means that you're not a Christian and God doesn't love you," I said as I finished up my talk. "God loves each of us and our ways of worshiping Him. It's not always going to look the same. And if you aren't a Christ follower, don't let those who are keep you from considering it. Not all Christians worship or praise in the same way. We're different, and that's OK. You can still be a Christian and not be what you see other people doing during prayer at chapel."

When I finished sharing the message God laid on my heart, they clapped. That was a huge thing for this group of ten seniors. Their enthusiasm was typically non-existent. But then one of my seniors, who was pretty outspoken about detesting most Christians, said, "I just got more from what you said than anything I've heard in chapel all year."

Part of me didn't want to share that. I don't want to hurt the chaplain or anyone else who had spoken in chapel that year. They had put their heart and soul into presenting to those kids. However, the fact of what he said completely drove home the point I made to my students: the point they so eagerly accepted and understood. My overall point was this: Christians don't all look the same. We're not supposed to. Yes, we should each carry Christ's love, and we should live God-centered lives, but how we do that is going to look different for different personalities.

It's tough. If the Christians you're surrounded by all act the same way and that's just not your personality, it can be discouraging. And from the discussions we had in class, I discovered that it can be especially discouraging for teens. They think, "I'll never be like that. That's just not me to do that or say that." More thoughts follow along the lines of: "Maybe I'm not a Christian." Their hyped-up Christian classmates inadvertently make them feel inadequate. They attribute the problem to their "level" of Christianity when in reality it's more of a personality difference.

I'm not saying anyone needs to "tone it down," but people who aren't like that need to know that it's OK. You can still have an awesome relationship with Christ without being so eccentric.

I also shared with the students the number one way that I've shared Christ with people: love. Simply put, love. Love people. Forgive people. Show grace towards people. Have mercy and compassion for people. I've never had someone say to me, "Natalie, thank you for telling me that I need Jesus. It's made me want to be a Christian." But I have had people say, "Thank you for loving me and for loving others as unconditionally as possible. I know this is because you're a Christian, and that helped lead me to Christ."

"And over all these virtues put on love, which binds them all together in perfect unity. Let the peace of Christ rule in your hearts, since as members of one body you were called to peace. And be thankful." Colossians 3:14-15

We're different. God wants us to be different. While Christian organizations tend to be flooded with similar personality types, sometimes you need a misfit who can reach out to the people who are different. I was definitely a misfit that year in Uganda. There were others, too.

CLOUDY BLESSING: Spiritual Gifts

"I'm not like them" was a legit statement to make about how I felt when I compared myself to many of my co-workers. Thank God for that. If I was exactly like them, I wouldn't have reached some of the students God used me to reach that day in class. The same goes for them—God used those people to reach the students I couldn't reach. God uses ALL of us.

"The body is a unit, though it is made up of many parts; and though all its parts are many, they form one body. So it is with Christ." 1 Corinthians 12:2

Don't hide your gifts behind a cloud. Use your God-given gifts to be a light for Jesus. Just because you don't worship like the Christians around you, doesn't mean you aren't as spiritual or important in the body of Christ. Do your thing. All that matters is what God thinks of you. And He thinks you're awesome.

46

The End is Approaching

I imagined myself getting off the plane in Detroit. After a long flight from Uganda to Amsterdam and an even longer flight from Amsterdam to Detroit, I'll have finally arrived in America. While Detroit wouldn't be my final stop, it would be my first steps on American soil in a year.

I imagined myself crying, falling to the ground, and kissing it. Yes, even the dirty floor of the Detroit airport.

I imagined myself running in slow motion towards the airport Starbucks with the Chariots of Fire theme song playing in my head. It would be so glorious. I would order my venti iced chai tea latte, and it would taste just as spectacular as I remembered.

It would be a grand return to my home country, and the thought of it made my stomach feel like it does when I ride down the huge hill of a roller coaster at an amusement park. It was scary, but it was also thrilling and wonderful.

I didn't have much time left in Uganda, and although I was as excited as ever about going home, I had to admit: I was horrified. As my time in Uganda was ending, the same question kept popping up in my mind: What if I've missed something? It sparked a long list of questions like, What if I haven't learned everything

I was supposed to learn? I've grown, but what if I haven't grown enough? What if I haven't given enough? I'd spent much of my time in Uganda battling depression. Was it all a waste?

I went to Africa to help. I wanted to make a difference, to follow God's calling, be it for a year or for the rest of my life. However, after a few months, I began to think that maybe God sent me to Uganda more for me than for others. Maybe He wanted me to grow. Maybe He wanted me to experience things that would forever change how I viewed the world. As the amount of time I had left in Uganda dwindled, I realized that wasn't entirely the case. I believed that I was there for other people as well as for myself. The only thing was that I wasn't there for the people I imagined I would be there for. Maybe I held and snuggled some babies who were HIV positive and didn't receive much love. Maybe I washed the feet of people who had jiggers. Those weren't the primary people God sent me to Africa for. He sent me there for my students.

And as I worried, "What if I've missed something?" I realized that God wouldn't let that happen.

"For this God is our God forever and ever: He will be our guide even unto death." Psalm 48:14

He was my guide the entire time. It's because of Him that I had the desire to hang out in my classroom with teenagers long after the final bell rang. It's because of His guidance that I had the right words to say to the struggling students who came to me for someone to listen. God wasn't going to let my time be wasted. Even though the bulk of my time was spent with students from places other than Uganda, that doesn't mean my time was in vain. Even if I was there to show God's love to just one student, even that was worth my time.

"Trust in the Lord with all your heart and lean not on your own understanding." Proverbs 3:5

I didn't miss anything in my time in Uganda. Because I trusted in the Lord and leaned on Him and not my own understanding, I couldn't go wrong.

On the last day of school, I had just a few days before I would head back to the United States. My roommate had already left, so I had the apartment to myself. It was strange to be alone, but I also kind of appreciated the time to reflect on the previous year of my life and how crazy it had been. At school, students came in and out of my room all day and after school, giving me thank-you cards and letters. I even received some cards and letters from fellow teachers.

"Your love for the kids you served at Redemption was always evident in the amount of time you spent with them. You have impacted their lives in ways only God knows!" one teacher wrote.

"You're beautiful. Thank you, Natalie, for all of the hard work you have done for this school. You've endured a lot this year, but I admire your relationship with Jesus and how strong you are in Him. People have hurt you, and you've stayed strong," another wrote.

Perhaps that was easy for teachers to say, but what about my students? As I struggled to convince myself that I had a positive impact on their lives, it was almost like their letters came from God, giving me confirmation that my time there was not wasted.

I don't share portions of their letters and cards to speak highly of myself. I share them to show how God used me in the middle of the biggest breakdown and depression of my entire life. I was as broken as I'd ever been, as insecure as I'd ever been, as mentally unstable as I'd ever been, and GOD STILL USED ME. He's so amazing.

"You're honestly one of the best teachers I've ever had. This year would have been completely different without you, and I'm going to miss you like crazy. You're super awesome, and you made this year so amazing!"

"This school year, you were my first friend. You were the first person I really talked to about my problems and about myself. You were more than willing to listen to my pointless stories. You were there to give me advice. You were there when my best friend wasn't and when my sister was too busy. You were there through everything, and I'm thankful."

"You deserve a thousand thank yous: for being a unique teacher, for sharing your experiences and even your mistakes, for giving great advice, for knowing when you've been at fault, for being open about your life, for being an inspiration to others. Thank you for your endless support and for the role you've played in my quest to find friends and God."

"You are the one I could always go to for advice. I knew I could always trust you. You are an incredible person and an amazing role model."

"Thank you for being the best teacher, role model, white person, and friend."

And finally, there was a double-sided, two-page letter from one of my male students, who poured out his heart. This was the letter that removed any doubt I had. This was the letter that God used to begin to heal my heart. Here's a portion of what that student wrote:

"I looked forward to devotions every day. Unlike everyone else who just told us what to do, you asked our opinions and gave your input. You led us to our conclusions which is far better than if you had just told us what to think. That is something I want to be great at in the future. You helped me listen to others opinions, even if they were stupid.

This probably sounds weird, but I want to be so into God and so close to Him that it makes people jealous. With the help you've given me, I think I can make it there.

At first, when I met you, I saw you as just another one of those Redemption teachers. You looked like a normal American. I know now that that was a dumb mistake. As the year progressed, I started to realize that you weren't here to teach, or because you thought it would be cool. You were here because God sent you. He knew I needed help, and He knew that you were the one to help me."

That student's words changed everything. It was almost like they took the hurt away. God did, in fact, send me to Uganda, if only for one year, and reading these words from co-workers and students was His way of letting me know that He was with me all along. He'll always be with me.

CLOUDY BLESSING: Reassurance

It might not always be immediate, it might not even be in this lifetime, but God will reveal to you why your suffering was worth the pain, and He'll show you how He was with you every step of the way. He will reassure you of everything you need reassured of.

47

The Hardest Goodbye

My friend Krista lived in a compound about a mile away from my first house in Uganda. One day we went to pick her up to go to the grocery store. Her gate, which remained locked and guarded of course, had a little viewing window so the guard could see who was arriving. But instead of seeing a guard peek out the small opening, I saw two tiny hands with painted pink fingernails dangle out. Then, I saw a sweet, tiny little face appear in the opening. She was so precious that I took a photo.

"Who is that?" I asked Krista when she got in the car.

"That's Florence, our day guard's daughter," she told me.

Time went on. Krista moved back to the United States early, and I ended up moving into her open room in the compound. I remember my first day going home to the new apartment after a day of teaching. I opened the gate and tiny little Florence came running towards me. You would think I was her best friend she hadn't seen in years. She would give me a giant hug, and behind her waddled Gideon, her little brother.

I thought it was because I was new, but as it turned out, that's how I was greeted every single day- with love and hugs from two of the cutest kids in all of Uganda.

I quickly learned that Florence loved to dance. She would twirl for me, hop around, sing and dance for as long as I would watch. And she would always say, "Look!" in her little accent, which actually made it sound like she was saying, "Luke!" She spoke very little English, but enough that I could tell her every day that she was beautiful, and she would reply, "Yes!"

Florence loved having her picture taken, and she especially loved being in videos. We had so much fun with my camera and computer sitting on my balcony and being silly. I also enjoyed my time with Giddy (Gideon), even though he was prone to peeing on our front porch. His goofy smile and giggle always made up for it.

I loved Florence so much that I would have happily brought her home with me to America, but Florence wasn't an orphan. She wasn't without a family. Her entire family actually lived on our compound in a "house" no larger than the size of my bedroom. She's got a mother and a father who have gone through the very worst in order to do what's best for her and Giddy. I learned that they weren't even Ugandan, but they were refugees from Congo. They arrived in Uganda on foot. They had seen two children die already as they made their escape from Congo. They had been through horrific things we can't even imagine.

On the worst of days, and I had my share of them in Uganda, Florence was the shining light that made me smile. Then, in December, Florence and her family left to return to Congo.

My heart was broken. Not only was I sad that I wouldn't be able to spend time with her, but I was horrified for the family's safety. The worst part was, I'd never know what happened to them. I'd never know if they made it back to Congo safely. I'd never know what happened to them if they did make it.

My initial response to the family returning to Congo was one of shock. Why on earth would they return to such a war-filled country? They escaped! Why return? I was somewhat relieved to learn that apparently things were getting better. Also, they couldn't afford to send Florence to school in Uganda, and in Congo, she would receive an education. If that was what was best for Florence, I was all for it.

December went on. It was sad for the first few days I came home and no one was there to greet me at the gate other than our new day guard, a young man who spoke no English. He didn't have even a fraction of the enthusiasm Florence and Giddy had. As a matter of fact, he had none.

On January 15, a few days after we'd returned to school from Christmas break, I came home from work and thought I saw a ghost. Florence was back. Giddy was back. Their entire family was back. I cried tears of joy as Florence jumped into my arms and gave me a huge hug. They were back, and my heart was so full.

For the next five months, I spent as much time with Florence as possible. I would paint her nails, we'd watch movies, we'd make videos, take pictures, and more. She was the bright spot in every single day I had in Uganda. So, when it was time to leave and move back to the United States in June, saying goodbye to Florence was the hardest.

I was already a blubbering mess after saying goodbye to a bunch of my students. My roommate had already left a few weeks prior, so it was just me. It's a moment I'll never forget. My bags were loaded into the van that would take me to the airport. It was evening, and the sun was setting. I said goodbye to Florence's mother, and then I said goodbye to Giddy. Then, it was time to say goodbye to Florence.

The toughest part about the entire interaction was that I couldn't explain what was happening. Her mother spoke very little English, and Florence only knew her numbers and letters in English. I hugged her so tightly and cried and cried. Not just tears, we're talking sobbing, almost throwing up crying. It was gut-wrenching, heartbreaking sobs of a broken heart in a way I'd never experienced before. Florence seemed confused, but I had no other choice than to give her one last hug and get in the van to leave. Saying goodbye to Florence was one of the hardest things I've ever done. I didn't think I'd ever see her again.

CLOUDY BLESSING: Relationships

"Blessed are those who mourn, for they will be comforted." Matthew 5:4

Life is filled with tough goodbyes, but that shouldn't stop us from finding people to love. The goodbyes will be heartbreaking, but God will comfort us through the pain. We should thank Him for the relationships we have in life. As you shed your tears in the middle of a goodbye, remember the One who is holding you close.

48

Returning Home

I started the journey out just me and God, in an airport, going somewhere new. Things were ending almost the same way. It was just me and God, in an airport. But we weren't going somewhere new. We were going home, to the good 'ole U.S. of A. It wasn't somewhere new.

Or was it?

After a tumultuous year in Uganda, who was I? Was I a better person? A worse person? I had no clue, and I wouldn't really know until I was back on American soil, reintegrated into the culture I'd known for 32 years. I'd had many missionaries tell me that going back home was sometimes more difficult than leaving. Having experienced a year in Uganda, nothing at home would look or feel the same.

I sat at my gate at the Entebbe airport in Uganda with a few hours to kill. There's not much of anything to do there, so I sat alone with my thoughts. My eyes hurt from crying the entire hour-drive to the airport after my heartbreaking goodbye to Florence.

"I just want some McDonalds!" I heard a teenage voice near me say. I looked over and saw a group of about a dozen American teenagers and a few adults in matching t-shirts. Their shirts told me that they'd just finished a mission trip. It was a week-long mission trip to Uganda.

"I want some Starbucks!" another said.

"I just want a hot shower!" one of the grownups said, and everyone laughed.

"I miss Godfrey already," one of the boys said. "I'll probably never see him again."

Instead of empathizing with them, I was a little angry. I hadn't had McDonalds or Starbucks in a year. I hadn't had a hot shower in a year. Whoever Godfrey was, he had likely known him for a week. I knew Florence for a year. Who were they to miss America after only a week? Who were they to even suggest that they "experienced" Uganda, when they were only there for a week?

I had to check myself. Or maybe it was the Holy Spirit. It was definitely the Holy Spirit. You can't escape the Holy Spirit when there's something you need to be reminded of. So right there in the airport, the Holy Spirit shut me up.

The Holy Spirit reminded me of two important things.

The first was that I used to go on short-term mission trips. My first was in Niger in 2009, then Nicaragua in 2011. In 2013, I went to Zambia. While the things we did on those trips likely weren't completely life-changing for the people we served, they certainly were for me. They grew my heart for missions, and had I not gone on those trips, I might not have moved to Uganda. God works in the lives of those who take mission trips in ways we might never see. Maybe one of those girls missing McDonalds would one day return to Uganda as a full-time missionary. Maybe she'd come back as a nurse. Maybe the trip participants would grow up to be big donors to support missionaries overseas. I had no idea how

202

God would use their short-term trip for something greater in the future.

Then, the Holy Spirit laid a big one on me: who was I to think I was so much better than them because I'd spent a year in Uganda, when I was surrounded by non-Ugandans who had lived there for decades. My measly little year was nothing compared to the families I met who moved there as a young couple and then had all their children there. Some of them will even retire there.

As I was having these thoughts, one of the teen girls caught me staring at them. Since the Holy Spirit had quieted my soul, I smiled, and she smiled back.

Before I knew it, I was on the plane and headed home. I was too tired and emotionally drained to cry again, so I spent most of my flights fast asleep. Somehow, all of my flights were bumped up, and I'd be getting back to Fort Wayne, Indiana about three hours earlier than planned. My layover in Amsterdam was so short that I didn't have time to let anyone know. I would have to do that when I landed in Detroit.

But when I landed in Detroit, I didn't have a working American cell phone I could use to call my parents, and I wasn't sure pay phones still existed. Even if they did, I didn't have any coins or cash. However, that would have to wait. What I needed first was some Starbucks. I ordered myself a venti iced chai latte and sipped it down so quickly that it almost made me sick. Of course, this was after I took a selfie with it and posted it on Instagram with the caption, "Guess who's in Detroit?"

I finally came across some modern payphones where I could pay with a credit card, and I called my parents. "I'm in Detroit! And I'll be home three hours early! I hope you can still come pick me up at the airport!" They were ecstatic, and said they would be there.

For that final flight, I was too excited to sleep. The idea of getting off of a plane and running into my parents' arms was too overwhelming. And when it finally did happen, it was just as incredible as I had imagined. I was home.

I hustled through the small, yet busy, Fort Wayne International Airport, searching for my parents. Sure enough, they were standing just outside security, wearing matching U.S.A. t-shirts and holding flowers. The three of us embraced and shed a few tears. There's no place like home.

I wanted my first meal back in the U.S. to be a Big John sandwich from Jimmy John's. As we drove there, I was amazed at how acclimated I had become to driving on the left side of the road. It was so strange to see everyone driving on the right side of the road. I even gasped a few times when we would make turns, and I feared we were pulling into the wrong lane. It's amazing how just a year had completely changed my brain to think of what was "normal."

Nothing fully prepared me for what was to come emotionally, though. I had changed so much that even my best friend, who was my rock the entire time I was in Uganda, ended up feeling like a stranger to me when we got together in person. I thank God for her and the role she played in my story as I battled so much overseas, but I am saddened that we end up growing apart.

There were other friendships that fell apart. Other friendships were strengthened. I spent another six months spitting up blood. I spent almost a year trying to find the right job.

I almost expected things to be incredible when I returned. God had sent me to Africa so I could be torn apart and put back together to better serve Him, that I was sure of. But I expected that to be immediate, and it was not. I expected the healing from my time in Uganda to be immediate, and it was not. I wouldn't find the true closure I desired until I returned to Uganda four years later. That would be my season of healing.

CLOUDY BLESSING: Seasons

"There is a time for everything, and a season for every activity under the heavens: a time to be born and a time to die, a time to plant and a time to uproot, a time to kill and a time to heal, a time to tear down and a time to build, a time to weep and a time to laugh, a time to mourn and a time to dance, a time to scatter stones and a time to gather them, a time to embrace and a time to refrain from embracing, a time to search and a time to give up, a time to keep and a time to throw away, a time to tear and a time to mend, a time to be silent and a time to speak, a time to love and a time to hate, a time for war and a time for peace." Ecclesiastes 3:1-8

Healing comes in God's perfect timing and can't be rushed. He knows the perfect time and season for healing your heart. Sometimes it's difficult to see a season as a blessing, especially when there's pain involved. But once the clouds are gone, once you can see clearly, you see the blessing of each and every season.

49

Return to Uganda

*O*ur church is going to Uganda this summer. We should go.

It was a text from my dad, who was in his early 70's at the time and hadn't been on a mission trip since we went to New Mexico 25 years prior.

He continued: *We could stay a few days extra and you could show me around Kampala where you used to live.*

Sure enough, we figured out the finances and signed up. My dad and I were going to Uganda, four years after I had left. I decided to start sponsoring a child through the organization we'd be going with, One More Child. Her name was Grace, and I'd get to meet her while we were there.

I was going back to Uganda. Back to the place that broke me. Back to the place where I started spitting up blood, where I was in a car accident, where I was mugged, where there are terror threats, where I was so depressed that I considered ending my own life. Back to Uganda. I had been through so much there. I still had some unresolved feelings about my time there. And, naturally, there was also the fear that whatever caused me to spit up blood for a year and a half would do the same to me if I returned. OK, so maybe that was mainly my mom who worried about that.

It was July 2018, and my dad and I were headed to Uganda. We'd meet up with the team in Atlanta, fly to Amsterdam, make a quick stop in Rwanda, and then we'd land in Entebbe. It was nearly the exact path I took when I moved there in 2013.

We hit it off with our team almost immediately. There was another father-daughter duo, some college girls, and a few singles. I could tell right away that it would be one of the best mission teams I'd ever been a part of. And at that point, I had been on six international mission trips.

We landed in Entebbe late at night and made the hour drive into Kampala where we checked into our hotel. I roomed with a girl named Ashley who had taken the trip the year before. Her enthusiasm about all we were about to experience was so encouraging. I had a feeling that this trip was going to be unlike any other.

And it was.

The next morning, we left the hotel, and we left Kampala. My dad was overwhelmed at the chaos that surrounded us as we drove through the city. He took lots of pictures and videos, and kept saying, "You drove in this mess?" It was hard for even me to believe.

Many hours later, we arrived in Kamonkoli, the village we'd be staying in for the following week. I instantly fell in love. We were about 135 miles from Kampala with no unruly traffic or towering buildings. We were in the heart of Uganda, surrounded by nature and how God created the Pearl of Africa to be. The children in the village stole our hearts, and the adults became our friends. We helped at the school, we delivered supplies to families who had no access to them, and I even taught an adult Sunday School class (with the help of a translator) at church on Sunday, and I did it all with my dad by my side. I fell in love with Uganda all over again, and it was like all of my negative experiences there were fading away.

It was our second day there that we got to meet Grace, my sponsor child. Grace was so incredibly grateful to meet me and my dad that she knelt in front of us as if we were a king and queen. This was her way of showing respect and appreciation. I scooped her up and hugged her, and she returned the love. I had learned of Grace's story. She was close to death due to having HIV and had no medical care. The organizations that were supporting Kamonkoli and its children intervened and got her the help she needed. My sponsorship would assure she could stay in school and get an education, on top of receiving necessities like clothing and food.

When our week was over, I was sad to leave Grace. I was also encouraged by all of the great work the missionaries were doing, and continue to do, there. While Grace's health will always be a concern, as well as other dangerous possibilities like child mutilation and sacrifice, I am comforted in knowing she is well taken care of.

At the end of the mission trip, our amazing team of new friends dropped my dad and I off at our AirBNB in Kampala before heading to the airport. Dad and I were going to spend a few days in Kampala where I would show him the school, where I lived, where I shopped, and even where I had my car accident.

On the afternoon that we visited the school, I met up with a couple I was friends with who still lived in Kampala. We saw their house and met their children, who had been born since I left four years prior.

"I know where Florence lives, do you want to go see her?" my friend asked me.

I nearly screamed, "YES!"

Florence and her family had left the compound and now had their own home. It wasn't much larger than their tiny space on our compound, but at least it was their own. Before I even got to see Florence, her mom showed me a framed school picture of Florence they had nailed to the wall. My sweet girl looked so grown.

I wasn't sure if Florence would remember me, and I was quite certain Giddy wouldn't. So I came prepared with a photo album of all the wonderful pictures we had taken together back when we lived on the same compound.

Florence's mom took us on a walk to try and find her. Sure enough, there was Florence. She was, of course, taller and even seemed shy, quite the opposite of how I knew her as a five-year-old little girl four years earlier. I pulled out the photo album, and we looked through the pictures. She smiled and even showed some of her friends the photos. They giggled when they saw the photos of little Giddy.

Florence and I got a few pictures taken together. I let her keep the photo album, and it was time to go. While I'm still not sure how much she remembered, it certainly did my heart good to see her family doing well.

My trip became even more meaningful when I met up with a former student: Samuel. Samuel was the senior who was also an atheist. That had changed since I left and he lovingly shared his testimony with me at a table in as I sipped a Stoney. He thanked me for playing a part in him finding Christ, even if it took a few years for him to come around. He was a changed young man. Before we parted ways, he took my hands and prayed for me while I cried tears of joy. It was a beautiful reminder that no one is ever so far gone that they can't be moved and changed by the love of Christ.

After dad and I battled Kampala insanity for a few days, we were definitely ready to go home. I was reminded of how stressful life in Kampala is. I relearned how a trip to the store is such an ordeal because of travel and traffic. No task is simple in Kampala.

Before we left Uganda, I took it all in. I could immediately see why I struggled so much that year I lived there. The atmosphere of Kampala alone could be catastrophic to anyone with anxiety, something I have battled for years. Add to that the fact that I spit up blood the entire time, had a car accident, and was thousands of miles away from loved ones, and it made for a pretty chaotic year. A therapist I saw years later told me I likely suffered PTSD from everything that happened there. I think she was spot on.

CLOUDY BLESSING: Healing

If I did, indeed, suffer from PTSD, that didn't mean God wouldn't use my trauma for good. He certainly did, and I see evidence of it often. When I left Uganda this time, my heart was happy and at peace. I loved Uganda again. I fell back in love with a country that deserves endless love. I was reminded of the Ugandan people, who are so loving and welcoming. I experienced the closure I needed, even though it took four years to get there. God's timing for my closure and healing was perfect.

"Therefore, if anyone is in Christ, the new creation has come. The old has gone, the new is here." 2 Corinthians 5:17

It would take that trip back to Uganda, four years later, to get the healing my heart needed. Don't give up on finding the healing you need. In God's perfect timing, it will happen.

50

I Had a Dream I Moved to Africa

I had a dream I moved to Africa, and my life was a different story. I helped orphans, the poor, and refugees, and I always gave God the glory. I lived in a hut in a village. I wore long skirts that never showed my knees. Never went to a mall or swimming. Entertainment was under the trees. The locals often thanked me. God used me to do His will. I made sure people got food and water. That every African had his or her fill. I had a dream I moved to Africa, and then that dream came true. It was nothing like the dream I had, but God, He always knew.

I literally moved to Africa. God asked me to teach some teens. I visited malls and swimming pools and ate more than just rice and beans.

Spent time with all my students, I spent less with the orphans and poor. God told me this was what He wanted. He said, "Natalie, that's what you're here for."

I thought teaching was my "in" that would get me to Africa like my dream. But God wanted me there to teach. He wanted me there for the teens.

I accepted His holy mission. There were tears, and there was fun. And before I even realized it, the mission was already done.

My classroom was nearly empty. My bedroom was no longer a reflection of me. The sunrise I saw on Monday could be the last one in Africa I ever saw.

My bags were packed, goodbyes were said, and I was crying as I waited for my plane. God comforted me. He gave me peace. He said, "We may do this again."

I had a dream I moved to Africa, a dream made true by God. African souvenirs all over my house. It certainly looks rather odd.

It feels like it didn't happen, almost feels like I was never even gone. Or maybe I just went for a week or two, but definitely not for that long.

I had a dream I moved to Africa. God wanted me there, that I can see. And now that I'm back in America, I'm still exactly where He wants me to be.

CLOUDY BLESSING: A Lifetime of Wisdom

While my insecurities and anxiety often clouded my vision of the truth, God still used every moment to teach me a lesson. Do what you must to clear away the clouds, and accept the abundant blessings God has for you.